The Art of Worldly Wisdom

CURRENCY
DOUBLEDAY

New York   London   Toronto   Sydney   Auckland

Baltasar Gracián

The Art *of*

Worldly

Wisdom

A Pocket Oracle

Translated by Christopher Maurer

A CURRENCY BOOK

PUBLISHED BY DOUBLEDAY
a division of Bantam Doubleday Dell Publishing Group, Inc.
666 Fifth Avenue, New York, New York 10103

CURRENCY and DOUBLEDAY
are trademarks of Doubleday,
a division of Bantam Doubleday Dell Publishing Group, Inc.

Book design by Chris Welch

Library of Congress Cataloging-in-Publication Data

Gracián y Morales, Baltasar, 1601–1658.
[Oraculo manual y arte de prudencia, English]
The art of worldly wisdom : a pocket-oracle / Baltasar Gracián ;
translated by Christopher Maurer. — 1st ed.
        p.   cm.
Translation of: Oraculo manual y arte de prudencia.
1. Maxims.   I. Maurer, Christopher.   II. Title.
P06398.G307   1991
868'.302—dc20   91-40712
                                                 CIP

ISBN 0-385-42131-1

5   7   9   10   8   6

Introduction

The Art of Worldly Wisdom: A Pocket Oracle is a book of strategies for knowing, judging, and acting: for making one's way in the world and achieving distinction and perfection. It is a collection of three hundred aphorisms too delicious not to share with friends and colleagues, too penetrating not to hide from enemies and rivals. Its ideal reader is someone whose daily occupation involves dealing with others: discovering their intentions, winning their favor and friendship, or (on the other hand) defeating their designs and "checkmating their will." Like all aphorisms, these are meant to be read slowly, a few at a time.

The *Pocket Oracle* revolves around a duality dear to the seventeenth century and to our own: it sees life as warfare involving both being and seeming, both appearance and reality. It provides advice not only for modern "image makers" and "spin doctors," but also for the candid: for those who insist that *substance*, not *image*, is what really matters. "Do, but also seem," is Gracián's pithy advice (aphorism 130). It assumes that good people are those most easily duped (21)—sheep in the midst of wolves—and it teaches us to temper the innocence of the dove with the wisdom of the serpent, governing ourselves according to the way people are, rather than the way they would like to be or to appear.

The *Oracle* has spoken in many tongues, has been heard with admiration and greeted with praise. It was imitated by La Rochefoucauld (who learned of it in the salon of his friend Mme de Sablé), valued by writers as diverse as Joseph Addison and Friedrich Nietzsche, and lovingly translated into German by Arthur Schopenhauer. Nietzsche observed that "Europe has never produced anything finer or more complicated in matters of moral subtlety,"[1] and Schopenhauer believed the *Oracle* "absolutely unique"

It teaches the art which all would fain practice, and is therefore a book for everyone; but it is especially fitted to be the manual of those who live in the great world, and peculiarly of young people who wish to prosper in that world. To them it gives at once and beforehand that teaching which they could otherwise only obtain through long experience. To read it once through is obviously not enough; it is a book made for constant use as occasion serves—in short, to be a companion for life.[2]

What sort of person composed these strategies for perfection? The voice that emerges from the *Oracle* is not, as some have argued, an entirely cynical, Machiavellian one. Baltasar Gracián (1601–1658), a worldly Jesuit priest, felt undying hatred for human folly. But the *Oracle* insists on the perfectability of man and the capacity of goodness, assisted by art, to triumph over evil.[3] It is true that in the *Oracle* perfection depends not upon religious revelation (God appears only rarely in these pages) but upon human resources and industry: attentiveness, mastery of one's emotions, self-knowledge, and other forms of prudence. There is, however, nothing irreligious or overly "pessimistic" about this emphasis on human reason. It was, after all, from St. Ignatius of Loyola, the founder of his order, that Gracián learned aphorism 251: "Use human means as though divine ones didn't exist, and divine means as though there were no human ones." In the *Oracle*, Gracián has all but ignored "divine" means, aware of Ignatius' advice and of the Spanish proverb it elaborates on: "Pray to God, but hammer away . . ."[4] Gracián assumes, without saying so, that God helps those who help themselves.

What is disconcertingly "modern" about this book

is the apparent subordination of ethics to strategy.[5] Moral generalizations, the immutable "hard rules" of ethics, yield, in these pages, to the conviction that to reach perfection one must adapt to circumstance. To achieve Gracián's *prudencia* (wisdom or prudence) one avoids generalities—among them, generalizations about morals. The *Oracle* bids us to speak the truth but to administer it skillfully, with a touch of artifice (210); the "most practical sort of knowledge lies in dissimulation" (98). We are to be "learned with the learned, saintly with saints . . . observe [others'] temperaments and adapt [ourselves] accordingly" (77). The wise are as mutable as Proteus. But even mutability and dissimulation must not harden into guiding principles. Gracián's insistence on adaptability, on metamorphosis and camouflage, reveals (an Italian philosopher reminds us) a poignant sense of man's fragility and vulnerability.[6]

Nor can Gracián be accused of indifference to the spiritual or material well-being of others. Avoid fools, he tells us repeatedly, but beyond that his injunctions are clear: "Speak what is very good, do what is very honorable" (202). "Know how to do good": little by little, with moderation (255). "Love, if you would be loved." Friendship is a recurrent theme, both here and in Gracián's other works, as it was in his life, and so is conversation. As for the "pessimism" of which he is often accused, the concept is anachronistic.

What many of us call "optimism"—a belief that people are basically good and that things will turn out for the best—Gracián would have regarded as a hoax of the imagination: "Hope is a great falsifier. Let good judgment keep her in check" (19).

Like other moralists of his age, from Francis Bacon and Jeremy Taylor to Francisco de Quevedo, Gracián labored painfully toward *desengaño*, the state of total "disenchantment" or disillusionment in which one gains control of one's hopes and fears, overcomes deceitful appearances and vain expectations, and weans oneself from false worldly values. Much of the *Oracle*, with its insistence on curbing the imagination, concerns strategies for reaching that bittersweet beatitude. To entertain no illusions about things or people was a large part of wisdom. The modern notions of pessimism and optimism seem shallow in comparison. Optimism would have seemed out of place, anyway, in seventeenth-century Spain—the Spain painted by Veláquez and Zurbarán—a kingdom in social turmoil and political decline. Like Quevedo, Gracián had the sense that his country's moral strength was waning. From time to time we hear a melancholy, unmistakably elegiac sigh: "Good conduct has departed, debts of gratitude now go unpaid, and few people give others the treatment they deserve . . ." (280). Only strategy—incessant plotting against one's own weaknesses and those of others—allows us to push forward to perfection. "It takes more to make one sage today than it did to make the seven of Greece" (1).

What of Gracián's own life, his own struggle toward worldly wisdom? It was not, as so many have written, an entirely uneventful one. He was born in 1601 in Belmonte, a village in Aragón,[7] not far from the birthplace of the great Latin satirist Martial, a coincidence which must have delighted him (Gracián's allegorical novel *El criticón*, or *The Master Critic*, is one of the most forceful satires ever written by a Spaniard). As an adolescent he studied philosophy and letters in Toledo and Zaragoza and in 1619, at the age of 18, entered the novitiate of the Jesuit order. For the remaining fifty years of his life Gracián labored as chaplain and confessor, preacher, professor, and administrator (he was rector and vice-rector of several Jesuit colleges). Though he never held an important position in public life, he kept company with those who did, and his aphorisms draw on long and careful observation of human behavior, both in peace and in warfare. As a young man, he served as confessor of the Viceroy of Aragón, the Neapolitan aristocrat Francesco Maria Carafa, accompanying him on several occasions to the court, and in 1646, in the bleakest days of the Revolt of Catalonia, Gracián served as chaplain of the royal armies that freed the Aragonese city of Lérida from the French. The only chaplain who neither fell ill nor was captured, Gracián went bravely to the front lines and, he says proudly in a letter, "exhorted the troops as they went into battle." The soldiers hailed him, he says, as "el Padre de la Victoria."

When he extols friendship as a pleasant way to acquire learning (11), he is thinking, no doubt, of blissful hours spent in the salon and library of his friend and protector Vicencio Juan de Lastanosa, six years younger than he, one of the wealthiest and most learned of seventeenth-century Spanish humanists. Lastanosa was patron of an important literary and cultural athenaeum, a true microcosm of all human learning, and it would be difficult to exaggerate his importance to Gracián. Gracián's first assignment after he took his vows was to the Jesuit College at Huesca, an ancient town to the northeast of Zaragoza. From the college it was only a few tempting steps to the Lastanosa mansion, an astoundingly rich Baroque "museum" of books and manuscripts, paintings (Titian, Dürer, Tintoretto, Ribera), sculpture, and objects of classical antiquity; there were, Lastanosa once wrote, "more than eight thousand coins and medals of Greek and Roman emperors . . . and two thousand cameos and stones from ancient rings."[8] Lastanosa was especially proud of his library, his collection of armor, and his botanical gardens, whose rare plants, trees, and shrubs were cared for by eight French gardeners, several of whom had held that post for more than half a century. There was even a small zoological garden: "in four caves, behind strong bars, were a tiger, a leopard, a bear and a lion. In a cage, two voracious ostriches." To Lastanosa's literary and cultural treasures, Gracián was granted access: an incalculable boon for one who thirsted for esthetic perfection and infallible taste, and hungered to "be vulgar in nothing" (28). It was Lastanosa who paid for the publication of several of Gracián's books, and many of the aphorisms of *The Art of Worldly Wisdom* may have been tried out for the first time on listeners in his salon.

The records of the Jesuits give us a glimpse of Gracián as priest and administrator, and he seems less stern, less forbidding in those pages than in these. In 1637, for example, he is rebuked for having been too lenient toward a fellow Jesuit guilty of "weakness" (*flaqueza*) with the opposite sex. A year later, the general of the Jesuit order suggests, from Rome, that Padre Gracián be reassigned: ". . . because he is a cross and a burden to his superiors, a source of problems and disturbances . . . , and because, displaying little prudence, he has been caring for the child of one who has left the order, asking for money to support him; and [also] because he has published a book, under the name of a brother of his."

The book alluded to is his first, *El Héroe*, *The Hero* (1637, 1639), an imaginary portrait of the perfect leader. Other treatises followed, most of them published (as the *Oracle* was) under the same pseudonym, Lorenzo Gracián, without permission from the Jesuit order: *El político* (1640, 1646), in which he ponders the political and moral greatness of King Ferdinand; *Arte de ingenio* (1642, 1648), a treatise on style and poetic conceit, with examples from a multitude of classical and Spanish authors; *El discreto* (1646), translated into English (1730) as *The complete gentleman, or a description of the several qualifications both natural and acquired, that are necessary to form a great man*), a book in the tradition of Castiglione's *Courtier*.[9]

Over the years Gracián was warned repeatedly not to publish his works without permission. So troubling was his continual disobedience that when he published the third and final volume of his masterpiece *El criticón*, a vast satirical allegory of human existence, he was removed from his chair of Sacred Scripture in Zaragoza and "exiled" to the country town where he died. From Rome came instructions to watch him closely, "to observe his hands," to "visit his room from time to time," and look over his papers. Were he to write anything against the Jesuits, he was to be locked up and forbidden the use of paper, pen, and ink. Not that his writings were regarded as heretical. It was somewhat unseemly for a Jesuit priest to write so brilliantly on worldly wisdom and on political behavior, but the Jesuits never accused Gracián of contradicting Catholic doctrine. What rankled his superiors was his persistent disobedience, and perhaps his nonchalance. "I am prohibited from publishing," he writes in 1653, "and have no lack of envious people. But I bear it all patiently, and am still able to eat lunch and dinner, to sleep, etc." Gracián's enemies cruelly exploited his problems with his superiors, and some of their allegations are delightful: in a sermon delivered in Valencia, Gracián is said to have told his listeners that he was reading from a letter he had just received from hell.

No doubt he was a difficult person, with a large dose of the stubbornness for which the Aragonese are famous. The Jesuits left a record of his prevailing humors: *"biliosus, melancolicus"* in 1628, *"colericus, biliosus"* in 1651 and, the year of his death, *"complexio colerica."* The author of *The Art of Worldly Wisdom*, a paean to prudence, is said to possess *ingenium bonum* (good intelligence) but, after 1645, his powers of judgment (*iudicium*), his prudence, and his experience of things are found less than normal, or barely satisfactory: *"iudicium infra mediocritatem"* (1651); *iudicium mediocre; prudentia non multa; experientia rerum mediocris"* (1655).[10] Were his fellow Jesuits right? Gracián may have shown poor judgment in publishing almost all of his works without authorization. But Time acquitted him. His works emerged unscathed, he won immortality, and no one remembers his accusers.

Even Gracián's style aroused animosity, and it continues to do so among those who have no time for brevity. He is one of the most laconic writers of the seventeenth century, a period when European humanists, heeding Justus Lipsius' call for brevity, delighted in Seneca and Tacitus and lost their taste for copious Cicero. Many of Gracián's stylistic habits are easy to recognize even in translation: antithesis and paradox; the constant use of ellipses; the concentration of meaning brought about by punning and other sorts of wordplay; the lack of connective tissue between one sentence—one *point*—and another (notice that there is often an abrupt transition between aphorism and commentary, and that the commentaries themselves often seem disjointed and fragmentary). These traits are more than idiosyncracies: they arise from a vision of human nature. The stylistic values reflected in these pages—wit, intensity, concision, subtlety—are also rules for wise living. For Gracián, living is a high art. Esthetic strategies correspond to moral ones. In other words, the author's relations with the reader are analogous to the reader's relations to those around him.[11] The author fences with the reader, withholds his meaning, disguises his intentions, avoids putting all of his cards on the table, keeps matters in suspense, and uses obscurity to awaken admiration and reverence: the reverence due an oracle. "The truths that matter most to us," Gracián writes self-reflectively, "are always half-spoken, fully understood only by the prudent" (25); "secrecy has the feel of divinity" (160).

Gracián does not mingle with the common reader, does not court his affection; he knows that affection spoils veneration and that familiarity breeds contempt (177). He does not want his writing and thinking to please the crowd (28, 245). He would have agreed with Luis de Góngora, Spain's great Baroque poet, who defended his *Solitudes* with these contemptuous words:

> It has been a matter of honor to me to make myself obscure to the ignorant, for that is what distinguishes the learned; to speak in a style that seems Greek to the ignorant, for precious pearls should not be cast before swine.[12]

Despite Gracián's authorial aloofness, the *Oracle* has delighted many thousands of readers. Perhaps that aloofness is a strategy for success. "Another trick," he writes, "is to offer something only to those in the know, for *everyone* believes himself an expert, and the person who isn't will want to be one. Never praise things for being easy or common: you'll make them seem vulgar and facile. Everybody goes for something unique" (150).

As with Góngora, it is pleasant to divine Gracián's meaning, lingering over a few aphorisms at a time. No doubt the ellipses and zigzags of his thought have contributed to the *Oracle*'s lasting appeal. "Don't express your ideas too clearly [. . .] To be valued, things must be difficult: if they can't understand you, people will think more highly of you" (253). The aphorisms are not arranged as a system. The Spanish critic Gonzalo Sobejano once observed that they come upon us with the chaos of life itself, reproducing "the chaotic randomness of pure experience."[13] This is surely the best of authorial defenses: "it is easy to kill the bird that flies in a straight line, but not the one that changes its line of flight" (17). Not that the book itself is organized chaotically. Gracián's approach is dialectical: as happens with popular proverbs, one aphorism offsets another, contradicting or complementing it, and moral phenomena are viewed from different perspectives. One fragment tells us how to perform a maneuver, another, how to defend ourselves from it.

As for brevity, it too is both an esthetic ideal and a strategy for survival. Say less, and you—as author or reader—will be less likely to be discovered, contradicted, proven wrong. "Speak as though you were writing your testament: the fewer words, the fewer lawsuits" (160). And "good things, if brief, [are] twice good." True, certainly, of translators' prefaces!

This translation follows upon seven previous English versions, only two of which I have been able to consult. The *Oracle*'s translators—one for each day of the week—are as follows: Anonymous, 1685; John J. Savage, 1702; Joseph Jacobs, 1892; Martin Fischer, 1934; Otto Eisenschiml, 1947; L. B. Walton, 1953; and Lawrence C. Lockley, 1967. To the Jacobs translation I have occasionally gone for help: not with questions about the meaning, but looking for solutions for Gracián's puns. "You may think you'll share pears, but you'll share only the parings" was the clever way Jacobs rendered an untranslatable sentence (237) about *peras* (pears) and *piedras* (stones), and I have gladly picked up those peelings.

Unlike that of Jacobs, this translation draws on the splendid critical edition of Miguel Romera-Navarro,[14] based on the only extant copy of the first edition (Huesca, 1647). Romera-Navarro sensed that his annotations would guide future translators, and that providence is cause for deep gratitude. I am grateful also to Harriet Rubin of Doubleday/Currency, an editor of uncommon taste, who believed that Gracián's delightful *Oracle* belongs in the pockets and hearts of contemporary readers.

Christopher Maurer
Vanderbilt University
May, 1991

1. From a letter to Peter Gast, 1884. In a note of 1873, Nietzsche writes: "In his experience of life, Gracián shows a wisdom and perspicacity that cannot be compared with anything today." See André Rouveyre, *Supplément a L'Homme de Cour de Baltasar Gracián* (Paris: Trianon, 1928), pp. 21–22.

2. M. E. Grant Duff, "Baltasar Gracián," *Fortnightly Review*, XXI (March, 1877), p. 328. Schopenhauer's translation was published posthumously in 1862.

3. On the context of Gracián's moral writings, see Monroe Z. Hafter, *Gracián and Perfection* (Cambridge: Harvard University Press, 1966).

4. "A Diós rogando, y con el mazo dando . . . ."

5. See Giovanni Bottiroli, "Lo splendore delle tenebre. Etica e strategia in Baltasar Gracián," *Quaderni Ibero-Americani*, 61–62 (December, 1987), pp. 208–15.

6. Ibid., p. 214.

7. A region in northeast Spain, bordering on Catalonia (to the east) and France (to the north).

8. On Lastanosa, and for further biographical information on Gracián, see E. Correa Calderón, *Baltasar Gracián. Su vida y su obra* (Madrid: Gredos, 1961). See also Virginia Ramos Foster, *Baltasar Gracián* (Boston: Twayne, 1975).

9. For an excellent bibliographical essay on these works, see Gonzalo Sobejano, "Gracián y la prosa de ideas," in Francisco Rico, ed., *Historia y crítica de la literatura española* (Barcelona: Crítica, 1983), Vol. III, Bruce Wardropper, ed., pp. 912–16.

10. For documentation on Gracián's life as a Jesuit, see Miguel Batllori, S.J., *Gracián y el Barroco* (Roma: Edizioni di Storia e Letteratura, 1958).

11. See the suggestive essay by B. Pelegrin, "Antithèse, métaphore, synecdoque et métonymie. Stratégie de la figure dans L'*Oráculo Manual* de Baltasar Gracián," *Revue de Littérature Comparée*, 3 (1982), pp. 339–50.

12. Alexander A. Parker, *Polyphemus and Galatea. A Study in the Interpretation of a Baroque Poem* (Edinburgh University Press, 1977), p. 17.

13. From a review of Dieter Kremers' study of Gracián's aphorisms. "Nuevos estudios en torno a Gracián," *Clavileño*, V, no. 26 (March–April, 1954), p. 24.

14. *Oráculo manual y arte de prudencia*, edición crítica y comentada por Miguel Romera-Navarro (Madrid: CSIC, 1954).

The Art of Worldly Wisdom

1 *All has reached perfection, and becoming a true person* is the greatest perfection of all.* It takes more to make one sage today than it did to make the seven of Greece. And you need more resources to deal with a single person these days than with an entire nation in times past.

2 *Character and intelligence.* The poles your talent spins on, displaying your gifts. One without the other brings only half of success. It isn't enough to be

---

*For Gracián, not everyone is a true "person" (*persona*). One becomes a "person" (and not merely a man or woman) by striving for moral perfection.

intelligent; you must also have the right character. The fool fails by behaving without regard to his condition, position, origin, or friendships.

3 *Keep matters in suspense.* Successes that are novel win admiration. Being too obvious is neither useful nor tasteful. By not declaring yourself immediately you will keep people guessing, especially if your position is important enough to awaken expectations. Mystery by its very arcaneness causes veneration. Even when revealing yourself, avoid total frankness, and don't let everyone look inside you. Cautious silence is where prudence takes refuge. Once declared, resolutions are never esteemed, and they lie open to criticism. If they turn out badly, you will be twice unfortunate. If you want people to watch and wait on you, imitate the divinity.

4 *Knowledge and courage take turns at greatness.* Because they are immortal, they can make you so. You are as much as you know, and if you are wise you can do anything. The uninformed person is a dark world unto himself. Judgment and strength: eyes and hands. Without courage, wisdom bears no fruit.

5 *Make people depend on you.* A god is made not by adorning the statue but by adoring it. He who is truly shrewd would rather have people need him than thank him. Vulgar gratitude is worth less than polite hope, for hope remembers and gratitude forgets. You will get more from dependence than from courtesy. He who has already drunk turns his back on the well, and the orange already squeezed turns from gold into mud. When there is no longer dependence, good manners disappear, and so does esteem. The most important lesson experience teaches is to maintain dependence, and entertain it without satisfying it. This can hold even a king. But don't carry it too far, leading others astray by your silence or making their ills incurable for your own good.

6 *Reach perfection.* No one is born that way. Perfect yourself daily, both personally and professionally, until you become a consummate being, rounding off your gifts and reaching eminence. Signs of the perfect person: elevated taste, a pure intelligence, a clear will, ripeness of judgment. Some people are never complete and are always lacking something. Others take a long time to form themselves. The consummate person—wise in speech, prudent in deeds—is admitted

to, and even desired by, the singular society of the discreet.

7 *Don't outshine your boss.* Being defeated is hateful, and besting one's boss is either foolish or fatal. Superiority is always odious, especially to superiors and sovereigns. The common sort of advantages can be cautiously hidden, as beauty is hidden with a touch of artful neglect. Most people do not mind being surpassed in good fortune, character, or temperament, but no one, especially not a sovereign, likes to be surpassed in intelligence. For this is the king of attributes, and any crime against it is lèse-majesté. Sovereigns want to be so in what is most important. Princes like to be helped, but not surpassed. When you counsel someone, you should appear to be reminding him of something he had forgotten, not of the light he was unable to see. It is the stars who teach us this subtlety. They are brilliant sons, but they never dare to outshine the sun.

8 *Not to be swayed by passions: the highest spiritual quality of all.* Let your superiority keep you from succumbing to vulgar, passing impressions. No mastery is greater than mastering yourself and your own pas-

sions: it is a triumph of the will. Even when passion affects your person, don't let it affect your position, least of all when the position is an important one. This is a wise way to avoid trouble and a shortcut to the esteem of others.

9 *Avoid the defects of your country.* Water shares the good and bad qualities of the beds through which it runs; people share those of the region where they are born. Some owe more than others to their mother country or city, for they were born under favorable skies. No country, not even the most refined, has ever escaped some innate defect or other, and these weaknesses are seized on by neighboring countries as defense or consolation. It is a triumph to correct, or at least dissimulate, such national faults. By doing so, you will be revered as unqiue among your people; for what is least expected is most valued. Other defects are caused by one's lineage, condition, occupation, and by the times. If all these defects come together in one person, and no care is taken to foresee and correct them, they produce an intolerable monster.

10 *Fame and fortune.* One is inconstant, the other firm. The latter helps us live, the former helps

us later. Fortune against envy, fame against oblivion. You can wish for fortune, and sometimes nurture it with your efforts, but all fame requires constant work. A desire for renown is born from strength and vigor. Fame is—has always been—the sister of giants. It always goes to extremes: monsters or prodigies, abomination or applause.

11 *Associate with those you can learn from.* Let friendly relations be a school of erudition, and conversation, refined teaching. Make your friends your teachers and blend the usefulness of learning with the pleasure of conversation. Enjoy the company of people of understanding. What you say will be rewarded with applause; what you hear, with learning. What draws us to others, ordinarily, is our own interest, and here that interest is ennobled. The prudent frequent the homes of courtly heroes: theaters of heroism, not palaces of vanity. Some are renowned for their learning and good judgment: oracles of all greatness through example and friendship. Those who accompany them form a courtly academy of gallant discretion and wisdom.

12 *Nature and art, material and labor.* All beauty requires help. Perfection turns into barbarism unless ennobled by artifice. Artifice rescues the bad and perfects the good. Nature often lets us down when we most need her; let us turn to art. The best disposition is unrefined without her, and perfection is only half itself without culture. People seem rough and rude without artifice. Perfection requires polish.

13 *Act on the intentions of others: their ulterior and superior motives.* Man's life on earth is a militia against *malicia*, or malice. Cunning arms itself with strategies of intention. It never does what it indicates. It takes aim deceptively, feints nonchalantly in the air, and delivers its blow, acting upon unforeseen reality with attentive dissimulation. To win the attention and confidence of others, it hints at its intention. But immediately it turns against that intention and conquers through surprise. The penetrating intelligence heads off cunning with close observation, ambushes it with caution, understands the opposite of what cunning wanted it to understand, and immediately identifies false intentions. Intelligence allows the first intention to pass by, and awaits the second one,

and even the third. Simulation grows even greater seeing that its guile has been penetrated, and tries to deceive by telling the truth. Changing strategies, it beguiles us with its apparent lack of guile. It bases its cunning on the greatest candor. But observation comes forward, sees through all this, and discovers the shadows that are cloaked in light. It deciphers intention, which is most hidden when most simple. Thus does the cunning of Python* struggle against the candor of the penetrating rays of Apollo.

14 *Both reality and manner.* Substance is not "stance" enough: you must also heed circumstance. The wrong manner turns everything sour, even justice and reason. The right one makes up for everything: it turns a "no" golden, sweetens truth, and makes even old age look pretty. The "how" of things is very important, and a pleasant manner captures the affection of others. A *bel portarse* is precious in life. Speak and act well and you will get out of any difficult situation.

*The huge serpent killed by Apollo at the foot of Parnassus.

15 *Surround yourself with auxiliary wits.* Things turn out well for the powerful when they are surrounded by people of great understanding who can get them out of the tight situations where their ignorance has placed them, and take their place in battling difficulty. It is singular greatness to use wise people: better than the barbaric taste of Tigranes,* who wanted to enslave the kings he conquered. This is a new way of mastering others, in what matters most in life: skillfully make servants of those whom nature made superior. We have little to live and much to know, and you cannot live if you do not know. It takes uncommon skill to study and learn without effort: to study much through many, and know more than all of them together. Do this and you will go to a gathering and speak for many. You will speak for as many sages as counseled you, and will win fame as an oracle thanks to the sweat of others. Choose a subject, and let those around you serve up quintessential knowledge. If you can't make knowledge your servant, make it your friend.

---

*King of Armenia (first century B.C.) who conquered Parthia and often appeared in public attended by the princes he had defeated.

16 *Knowledge and honorable intentions* ensure that your success will bear fruit. When understanding marries bad intention, it isn't wedlock but monstrous rape. Malevolence poisons perfection. When abetted by knowledge, it corrupts even more subtly. Superior talents given to baseness come to a bad end. Knowledge without judgment is double madness.

17 *Keep changing your style of doing things.* Vary your methods. This will confuse people, especially your rivals, and awaken their curiosity and attention. If you always act on your first intention, others will foresee it and thwart it. It is easy to kill the bird that flies in a straight line, but not one that changes its line of flight. Don't always act on your second intention either; do something twice, and others will discover the ruse. Malice is ready to pounce on you; you need a good deal of subtlety to outwit it. The consummate player never moves the piece his opponent expects him to, and, less still, the piece he *wants* him to move.

18 *Application and capacity.* Eminence requires both. When both are present, eminence outdoes itself. The mediocre people who apply themselves go further than the superior people who don't. Work makes worth. You purchase reputation with it. Some people are unable to apply themselves to even the simplest tasks. Application depends almost always on temperament. It is all right to be mediocre at an unimportant job: you can excuse yourself by saying you were cut out for nobler things. But to be mediocre at the lowest of jobs, rather than excellent at the highest, has no excuse at all. Both art and nature are needed, and application makes them complete.

19 *When you start something, don't raise other people's expectations.* What is highly praised seldom measures up to expectation. Reality never catches up to imagination. It is easy to imagine something is perfect, and difficult to achieve it. Imagination marries desire, and conceives much more than things really *are*. No matter how excellent something is, it never satisfies our preconceptions. The imagination feels cheated, and excellence leads more often to disappointment than to admiration. Hope is a great

falsifier. Let good judgment bridle her, so that enjoyment will surpass desire. Honorable beginnings should serve to awaken curiosity, not to heighten people's expectations. We are much better off when reality surpasses our expectations, and something turns out better than we thought it would. This rule does not hold true for bad things: when an evil has been exaggerated, its reality makes people applaud. What was feared as ruinous comes to seem tolerable.

20 *A person born in the right age.* People of truly rare eminence depend on the times. Not all of them had the times they deserved, and many who did were unable to take advantage of them. Some were worthy of better times, for not all goodness triumphs always. Things have their seasons, and even certain kinds of eminence go in and out of style. But wisdom has an advantage: she is eternal. If this is not her century, many others *will* be.

21 *The art of success.* Good fortune has its rules, and to the wise not everything depends upon chance. Fortune is helped along by effort. Some people confidently approach the door of Fortune, and

wait for her to go to work. Others are more sensible: they stride through that door with a prudent sort of boldness. On the wings of their courage and virtue, audacity spies luck and flatters it into effectiveness. But the real philosopher has only one plan of action: virtue and prudence; for the only good and bad fortune lie in prudence or rashness.

22 *Be well informed.* The discreet arm themselves with a store of courtly, tasteful learning: not vulgar gossip, but a practical knowledge of current affairs. They salt their speech with witticisms, and their actions with gallantry, and know how to do so at the right moment. Advice is sometimes transmitted more successfully through a joke than through grave teaching. The wisdom passed along in conversation has meant more to some than the seven arts, no matter how liberal.

23 *Don't have a single imperfection.* Few people live without some moral flaw or character defect, and they give in to it when it would be easy to cure. The prudence of others is grieved to see a universal, sublime talent threatened by a small defect: a single

cloud eclipses the sun. Defects are moles on the face of reputation, and malevolence is good at noticing them. It takes supreme skill to turn them into beauty marks. Caesar covered his defect with laurels.*

24 *Temper your imagination.* You must sometimes rein it in and sometimes encourage it. On imagination all happiness depends: it should be governed by good sense. Sometimes it behaves like a tyrant. It isn't content to speculate, but swings into action and takes over your life, making it pleasant or unpleasant, and making us unhappy or too satisfied with ourselves. To some it shows only grief: for imagination is a homespun henchman of fools. To others it promises happiness and adventure, gaiety and giddiness. It can do all this as long as it remains unchecked by prudence and common sense.

25 *Know how to take a hint.* Knowing how to reason was once the art of arts. It is no longer enough. One must also be a diviner, especially in matters where you can easily be deceived. You will never be intelligent unless you know how to take a hint. Some

*He hid his baldness under a crown of laurel.

people are diviners of the heart and sharp-eyed lynxes of others' intentions. The truths that matter most to us are always half spoken, fully understood only by the prudent. In matters that seem favorable, rein in your credulity. In those that seem hateful, give it the spur.

26 *Find each person's "handle," his weak point.* The art of moving people's wills involves more skill than determination. You must know how to get inside the other person. Each will has its own special object of delight; they vary according to taste. Everyone idolizes something. Some want to be well thought of, others idolize profit, and most people idolize pleasure. The trick is to identify the idols that can set people in motion. It is like having the key to someone else's desires. Go for the "prime mover," which isn't always something lofty and important. Usually it is something low, for the unruly outnumber the well ruled. First size up someone's character and then touch on his weak point. Tempt him with his particular pleasure, and you'll checkmate his will.

27 *Better to be intensive than extensive.* Perfection isn't quantity, but quality. Very good things have

always been small and rare; muchness brings discredit. Even among men, the giants are usually the dwarfs. Some praise books for their girth, as though they were written to exercise our arms, not our wits. Extension alone can never be more than mediocre, and the universal men who want to be in on everything are often in on nothing. Intensity leads to eminence and even—in matters of great importance—fame.

28 *Be vulgar in nothing.* Certainly not in your taste. What a wise person it was who did not want his things to please the many! The discreet never gorge themselves on vulgar applause. Some people are such puffed-up chameleons of popularity* that they enjoy the breath of the crowd more than the gentle breezes of Apollo. And not in understanding. Take no pleasure in the miracles of the many: they are nothing but quackery. The crowd admires common foolishness and places no stock in excellent counsel.

29 *Be righteous and firm.* Side with reason and do this so steadily that neither vulgar passion nor

*A symbol of vanity, the chameleon was thought to live on air.

tyrannical violence will make you stray from it. But where will we find such a Phoenix of equity? Few are devoted to righteousness. Many celebrate her, but few visit her. Some follow her until things get dangerous. In danger, the false disown her and politicians cunningly disguise her. She is not afraid to set aside friendship, power, and even her own good, and this is when people disown her. Clever people spin subtle sophistries and speak of their laudable "higher motives" or "reasons of security," but the truly faithful person considers deceit a sort of treason, is prouder to be steadfast than clever, and is always found on the side of truth. If he differs with others, it isn't because of any fickleness of his own, but because others have abandoned the truth.

30 *Don't occupy yourself with disreputable things*, even less with chimerical ones that bring more scorn than renown. Caprice has founded many sects, and the sane person should flee from all of them. There are people with extravagant tastes who embrace anything wise people repudiate. They take pleasure in any sort of eccentricity, and although this makes them well known, they are more often laughed at than renowned. Even when pursuing wisdom, the prudent ought to shun affectation and public notice, especially

in things that can make them look ridiculous. There is no use pointing out these pursuits one by one: common ridicule has already done so.

31 *Know the fortunate in order to choose them, and the unfortunate in order to flee from them.* Bad luck is usually brought on by stupidity, and among outcasts nothing is so contagious. Never open the door to the least of evils, for many other, greater ones lurk outside. The trick is to know what cards to get rid of. The least card in the winning hand in front of you is more important than the best card in the losing hand you just laid down. When in doubt, it is good to draw near the wise and the prudent. Sooner or later they will be fortunate.

32 *Be known for pleasing others*, especially if you govern them. It helps sovereigns to win the good graces of all. Ruling others has one advantage: you can do more good than anyone else. Friends are those who do friendly things. Some people are intent on not pleasing, not because it is burdensome, but simply out of nastiness. In everything they oppose the divine communicability.

33   *Know when to put something aside.* One of life's great lessons lies in knowing how to refuse, and it is even more important to refuse yourself, both to business and to others. There are certain inessential activities—moths of precious time—and it is worse to busy yourself with the trivial than to do nothing. To be prudent, it isn't enough not to meddle in other people's business: you must also keep them from meddling in yours. Don't belong so much to others that you stop belonging to yourself. You shouldn't abuse your friends, or ask them for more than they give on their own initiative. All excess is a vice, especially in your dealings with others. With this judicious moderation you will stay in the good graces of others and keep their esteem; and propriety, which is precious, will not be worn away. Retain your freedom to care passionately about the best, and never testify against your own good taste.

34   *Know your best quality*, your outstanding gift. Cultivate it and nurture all the rest. All people could have achieved eminence in something if only they had known what they excelled at. Identify your king of attributes and apply it in double strength.

Some excel at judgment and others at courage. Most people force their intelligence and achieve superiority in nothing. Their own passions blind and flatter them until—too late!—time gives them the lie.

35 *Weigh matters carefully*, and think hardest about those that matter most. Fools are lost by not thinking. They never conceive even the half of things, and because they do not perceive either their advantages or their harm they do not apply any diligence. Some ponder things backward, paying much attention to what matters little, and little to what matters much. Many people never lose their heads because they have none to lose. There are things we should consider very carefully and keep well rooted in our minds. The wise weigh everything: they delve into things that are especially deep or doubtful, and sometimes reflect that there is more than what occurs to them. They make reflection reach further than apprehension.

36 *Take the measure of your luck*: in order to act, and in order to commit yourself. This matters more than identifying your predominant humor and

understanding your physical makeup. It is foolish for
a forty-year-old to ask Hippocrates for health, and
even more foolish to ask Seneca for wisdom. It is a
great art to govern Fortune, either awaiting her (for
she sometimes takes her time) or taking advantage of
her (for she sometimes turns good), although you will
never completely understand her inconsistent behavior. If she has favored you, proceed with boldness, for
she often loves the daring and, like a dazzling woman,
the young. If you are unlucky, act not. Withdraw and
save yourself from failing twice. If you master her,
you have taken a great step forward.

37 *Know what insinuation is, and how to use it.*
It is the subtlest point in your dealings with others.
It can be used to test the wits and cunningly probe
the heart. Some insinuation is malicious, careless,
tinged with the herbs of envy, smeared with the poison of passion: an invisible lightning bolt that can
knock you from grace and esteem. Some people owe
their downfall to a single wounding, insinuating word.
Those who expelled them from power showed not the
slightest fear before an entire conspiracy of common
murmuring and singular malevolence. Other insinua-
tions—favorable ones—do the opposite, shoring up
our reputation. But we should catch these darts as

skillfully as they are hurled at us by evil intention: catch them carefully, await them prudently. A good defense requires knowledge. When we expect a blow we can ward it off.

38 *Quit while you're ahead.* All the best gamblers do. A fine retreat matters as much as a stylish attack. As soon as they are enough—even when they are many—cash in your deeds. A long run of good fortune is always suspicious. You're safer when good luck alternates with bad, and, besides, that makes for bittersweet enjoyment. When luck comes racing in on us, it is more likely to slip and smash everything to pieces. Sometimes Lady Luck compensates us, trading intensity for duration. She grows tired when she has to carry someone on her back for a long time.

39 *Know when things are at their acme, when they are ripe, and know how to take advantage of them.* All works of nature reach their point of full perfection. Before, they were gaining; from then on, waning. As for works of art, only rarely can they not be improved. People with good taste know how to enjoy each thing when it reaches perfection. Not everyone can, and not everyone who can knows how. Even the fruits of the understanding attain this ripeness. But you must know it in order to value and use it.

40 *Grace in dealing with others.* It is a great thing to win universal admiration, but even greater to win benevolence. Part of it is having a lucky star, but diligence is more important. One begins with the former and carries through with the latter. It isn't enough to be eminently gifted, though people often suppose it is easy to win affection when one has a reputation. Benevolence depends on beneficence. Do all sorts of good: good words and better deeds. Love if you would be loved. Courtesy is the way great people bewitch others. Reach for deeds and then for the pen. From the sword to the pen, for there is also grace among writers, and it is eternal.

41 *Never exaggerate.* It isn't wise to use superlatives. They offend the truth and cast doubt on your judgment. By exaggerating, you squander your praise and reveal a lack of knowledge and taste. Praise awakens curiosity, which begets desire, and later, when the goods seem overpriced, as often happens, expectation

feels cheated and avenges itself by running down the praised and the praiser. The prudent show restraint, and would rather fall short than long. True eminences are rare, so temper your esteem. To overvalue something is a form of lying. It can ruin your reputation for good taste, and—even worse—for wisdom.

42 *Born to rule.* It is a secret, superior force. It doesn't spring from bothersome artifice, but from a nature born to rule. Everyone succumbs to such a person without knowing why, recognizing the secret strength and vigor of innate authority. People like this have a lordly character: kings by merit, lions by natural right. They seize the respect, the heart, and even the minds of others. When blessed with other gifts, they are born to be political prime movers. They can accomplish more with a single feinting gesture than can others with a long harangue.

43 *Feel with the few, speak with the many.* Rowing against the current makes it impossible to discover the truth and is extremely dangerous. Only Socrates could attempt it. Dissent is taken as insult, for it condemns the judgment of others. Many take offense, whether on account of the person criticized or the one who applauded him. The truth belongs to the few. Deceit is as common as it is vulgar. You can never tell the wise by what they say in public. They speak not in their own voices, but in that of common stupidity, though deep inside they are cursing it. The sensible person avoids both being contradicted and contradicting others. He may be quick to censure, but he is slow to do so in public. Feelings are free; they cannot and should not be violated. They live in silent retirement and show themslves only to a few sensible people.

44 *Sympathy with the great.* One of the gifts of the hero is the ability to dwell with heroes. This ability, called sympathy, is a wonder of nature, both because it is so mysterious and because it is so beneficial. There are similar hearts and temperaments, and the effects of sympathy resemble those which vulgar ignorance attributes to magic potions. Not only can this sympathy help us win renown, it inclines others towards us and quickly wins their goodwill. It persuades without words, achieves without merit. There is active and passive sympathy,* and both kinds work wonders among people in high positions. It takes great

*Gracián's meaning is not entirely clear. Romera-Navarro believes "active sympathy" is that which elicits similar feelings in others, and "passive" that which does not.

skill to know them, distinguish between them, and take advantage of them. No amount of effort can take the place of this mysterious favor.

45 *Use, but don't abuse, hidden intentions*, and above all, don't reveal them. All art must be concealed, for it rouses suspicion, especially hidden intentions, which are hateful. Deceit is common, so be on your guard. But hide your caution from others, so as not to lose their confidence. When it becomes known, caution offends others and provokes vengeance, awakening unimagined evils. A reflective way of doing things will give you a great advantage. Nothing provides more food for thought. The greatest perfection of an action depends upon the mastery with which it is carried out.

46 *Temper your antipathy*. We hate some people instinctively, even before we are aware of their good qualities. And sometimes this vulgar, natural aversion is directed towards the eminent. Let prudence keep it in check: there is nothing more demeaning than to abhor the best people. It is as excellent to get along with heroes as it is disgraceful to treat them with antipathy.

47 *Avoid committing yourself to risky enterprises.* This is one of the chief goals of prudence. People of great talent keep well away from extremities. There is a long way to walk from one extreme to another, and the prudent stick to the middle ground. Only after long deliberation do they decide to act, for it is easier to hide oneself from danger than to overcome it. Dangerous situations place our judgment in jeopardy, and it is safer to flee from them entirely. One danger leads to another, greater one, and brings us to the edge of disaster. Some people are rash, because of their temperament or their national origin, and they are quick to commit themselves and place others in danger. But the person who walks in the light of reason sizes up the situation and sees that there is more courage in avoiding danger than in conquering it. He sees that there is already one rash fool, and avoids adding another.

48 *You are as much a real person as you are deep.* As with the depths of a diamond, the interior is twice as important as the surface. There are people who are all façade, like a house left unfinished when the funds run out. They have the entrance of a palace but the inner rooms of a cottage. These people have no place you can rest, though they are always at rest, for once they get through the first salutations, the conversation is over. They prance through the initial courtesies like Sicilian stallions, but immediately lapse into monkish silence. Words dry up when not refreshed by perennial springs of wit. Such people easily fool those who see things superficially, but not the sharp-sighted, who look inside them and find only emptiness.

49 *A person of sharp observation and sound judgment* rules over objects and keeps objects from ruling him. He plumbs the greatest depths, and studies the anatomies of other people's talent. No sooner does he see someone than he has understood him and judged his essence. With rare powers of observation he deciphers even what is most hidden. He observes sternly, conceives subtly, reasons judiciously: there is nothing he cannot discover, notice, grasp, understand.

50 *Never lose your self-respect* or grow too familiar with yourself. Let your *own* integrity keep you righteous. You should owe more to the severity of your own judgment than to all external precepts. Avoid what is indecorous, not because others will judge you harshly, but because you fear your own prudence. Grow to fear yourself and you will have no need of Seneca's imaginary witness.*

51   *Know how to choose.* Most things in life depend on it. You need good taste and an upright judgment; intelligence and application are not enough. There is no perfection without discernment and selection. Two talents are involved: choosing and choosing the best. There are many people with a fertile, subtle intelligence, rigorous judgment, both diligent and well informed, who are lost when they have to choose. They always choose the worst, as though they wanted to show their skill at doing so. Knowing how to choose is one of heaven's greatest gifts.

52   *Never lose your composure.* Prudence tries never to lose control. This shows a real person, with a true heart, for magnanimity is slow to give in to emotion. The passions are the humors of the mind,

*Your own conscience. Gracián is alluding to one of Seneca's *Moral Epistles*.

and the least excess sickens our judgment. If the disease spreads to the mouth, your reputation will be in danger. Master yourself thoroughly and no one will criticize you for being perturbed, either when things are at their best or at their worst. All will admire your superiority.

53 *Be diligent and intelligent.* Diligence is quick to carry out what intelligence has lingered over. Fools are fond of hurry: they take no heed of obstacles and act incautiously. The wise usually fail through hesitation. Fools stop at nothing, the wise at everything. Sometimes things are judged correctly but go wrong out of inefficiency and neglect. Readiness is the mother of luck. It is a great deed to leave nothing for the morrow. A lofty motto: make haste slowly.

54 *Act boldly but prudently.* Even hares tweak the beard of a dead lion. Like love, courage is no joking matter. If it yields once, it will have to yield again, and again. The same difficulty will have to be conquered later on, and it would have been better to get it over with. The mind is bolder than the body. So with the sword: let it be sheathed in prudence, ready for the occasion. It is your defense. A weak spirit does more harm than a weak body. Many people with eminent qualities lacked this brio, appeared to be dead, and were buried in their lassitude. Provident nature resourcefully joined the sweetness of honey with the sting of the bee. You have both nerves and bones in your body: don't let your spirit be all soft-ness.

55 *Know how to wait.* It shows a great heart with deep reserves of patience. Never hurry and never give way to your emotions. Master yourself and you will master others. Stroll through the open spaces of time to the center of opportunity. Wise hesitation ripens success and brings secrets to maturity. The crutch of Time can do more than the steely club of Hercules. God himself punishes not with iron hands but with leaden feet. A wonderful saying: "Time and I can take on any two." Fortune gives larger rewards to those who wait.

56 *Think on your feet.* Good impulses spring from a happy readiness of spirit. For such a spirit there are no tight spots, no troubling chance occur-rences, only vivacity and brio. Some think much, and then do everything wrong, and others get everything

right without any forethought at all. Some people have reserves of antiperistasis.* Difficulties bring out the best in them. They are monsters who succeed spontaneously and err whenever they have thought about something. What doesn't occur to them immediately will never occur to them, and there is no use thinking about later. Quickness wins applause, for it reveals prodigious talent: subtlety in thought, prudence in deeds.

57 *Thoughtful people are safer.* Do something well, and that is quick enough. What is done immediately is undone just as fast, but what must last an eternity takes that long to do. Only perfection is noticed, and only success endures. Deep understanding achieves eternities. Great worth requires great work. So with metals: the most precious of them takes longest to be refined, and weighs most.

58 *Adapt to those around you.* Don't show the same intelligence with everyone, and don't put more effort into things than they require. Don't waste your

Antiperistasis: Opposition by which the quality opposed acquires strength.

knowledge or merit. The good falconer uses only the birds he needs. Don't show off every day, or you'll stop surprising people. There must always be some novelty left over. The person who displays a little more of it each day keeps up expectations, and no one ever discovers the limits of his talent.

59 *End well.* If you enter the house of Fortune through the door of pleasure, you will leave through the door of sorrow, and vice versa. So be careful of the way you end things, and devote more attention to a successful exit than to a highly applauded entrance. Fortunate people often have very favorable beginnings and very tragic endings. What matters isn't being applauded when you arrive—for that is common —but being missed when you leave. Rare are those who are still wanted. Fortune seldom accompanies someone to the door. She is as courteous to those who are coming as she is rude to those who are going.

60 *Good judgment.* Some people are born prudent. They come into the world with an advantage —the good sense that is a natural part of wisdom—and they have already walked half the road to success. With age and experience their reason reaches complete maturity, and their judgment is tuned to its surroundings. These people hate any sort of whim that can tempt prudence, especially in matters of state, where total security is important. Such people as these deserve to steer the ship of state, either as helmsmen or as counselors.

61 *Eminence in what is best.* Amid different sorts of perfection, this is a rarity. There is no hero without some sublime quality. Mediocrity never wins applause. Eminence at some lofty pursuit redeems us from ordinary vulgarity, raising us to the exceptional. To be eminent in a lowly occupation is to be something at very little: the more comfort, the less glory. To be exceptional at superior things gives you a sovereign character: it wins admiration and gains the goodwill of others.

62 *Use the best instruments.* Some people want to be thought subtle because they use poor instruments. This is a dangerous sort of satisfaction and it deserves a fatal punishment. The worth of a prime minister never detracted from the greatness of his master. To the contrary, all the credit for success falls

upon its principal cause, as does criticism in the case of failure. It is superiors who win the renown. One never says "He had good, or bad, ministers," but "He was a good, or bad, craftsman." So choose carefully, examine your ministers. To them you are entrusting your immortal fame.

63 *The excellence of being first.* It is doubled when you are truly eminent. Other things being equal, the person who makes the first move has the advantage. Some people would have been as unique as the Phoenix in their occupations if others had not preceded them. Those who are first are the firstborns of fame, and the children who follow are left to file lawsuits for their daily bread. No matter how hard they try, they cannot elude the vulgar accusation that they are imitators. Prodigious, subtle people have always invented new ways to achieve eminence, provided that prudence makes their adventures safe. Using novelty, wise people have found room in the roster of heroes. Some people would rather be first in second class than second in first.

64 *Avoid grief.* It is both beneficial and wise to steer clear of troubles. Prudence will save you from

many: it is the Lucina* of good fortune and content. Don't give others hateful news unless there is a remedy, and be even more careful not to receive it. Some people's hearing is spoiled by the sweetness of flattery, others' by hearing bitter gossip, and there are people who cannot live without a daily dose of unpleasantness, like Mithridates with his poison.** Nor can you keep well by inflicting lifelong grief on yourself in order to please someone else, even if he is close to you. Never sin against your own happiness in order to please the person who counsels you and has nothing at stake in the matter. When giving pleasure to another involves giving grief to yourself, remember this lesson: better for the other person to feel grief now than for you to feel it later, and with no hope.

65 *Elevated taste.* You can cultivate it, as you can the intellect. Full understanding whets the appetite and desire, and, later, sharpens the enjoyment of possession. You can judge the height of someone's talent by what he aspires to. Only a great thing can satisfy a great talent. Large bites are for large palates,

---

*Roman goddess of childbirth; used as surname of Juno and Diana.
**King of Pontus, who, fearing his enemies would poison him, accustomed himself by taking daily doses of it.

lofty matters for lofty characters. Even the greatest excellences tremble before the person of refined taste, and the most perfect lose their confidence. Few things have perfection of the first magnitude: let your appreciation be sparing. Taste is acquired through contact with others. You make it your own through continual exercise. You are lucky if you can associate with someone with perfectly developed taste. But don't profess to be satisfied with nothing; it is a foolish extreme, more odious if from affectation than if from character. Some wish God had created another world and other perfections just to satisfy their own extravagant imagination.

66 *Take care to make things turn out well.* Some people scruple more over pointing things in the right direction than over successfully reaching their goals. The disgrace of failure outweighs the diligence they showed. A winner is never asked for explanations. Most people pay more attention to success or failure than to circumstances, and your reputation will never suffer if you achieve what you wanted to. A good ending turns everything golden, however unsatisfactory the means. It is an art to set aside art when you must do so to bring things to a happy conclusion.

67 *Choose an occupation in which you can win praise.* Most things depend upon the satisfaction of others. Esteem is to perfection what the zephyr is to flowers: breath and life. There are occupations that enjoy universal acclaim, and others that are more important but barely visible. The former are seen by all, and win common benevolence. The latter are rarer and require more skill, but are secret and barely perceived, venerated but not applauded. Among princes, the most celebrated are the victorious ones, and that is why the kings of Aragon were so acclaimed: as magnanimous conquerors and warriors. The great person should prefer celebrated occupations that all can see and share. Common suffrage will make him immortal.

68 *Make others understand.* It is more excellent than making them remember, for intelligence is much greater than memory. Sometimes you should remind other people, and other times counsel them about the future. Some people failed to do things that were ripe for doing simply because it never occurred to them. Let friendly advice point out the advantages. One of the greatest of gifts is to size up quickly what matters. When this is lacking, many successes go undone. Let the person who has light give it to others, and let those who lack it ask for it, the former with prudence, and the latter with discretion, merely dropping a hint. This delicacy is especially necessary when the person giving advice has something at stake. It is best to show good taste and to be more explicit only when insinuation is not enough. A "no" has already been given, and you can now search skillfully for a "yes." Most of the time things are not obtained because they were not attempted.

69 *Don't give in to every common impulse.* The great do not yield to every sort of passing thought. Part of prudence lies in reflecting about yourself: knowing or foreseeing your disposition, and moving towards the other extreme in order to balance art and nature. Self-correction begins with self-knowledge. There are monsters of impertinence who are always ruled by a certain humor, and their emotions vary accordingly. Tossed about by this vile imbalance, they go about their business in a self-contradictory way. Not only does this excess ruin their will, it also attacks their judgment, troubling their desire and under-standing.

70 *Know how to say "no."* You can't grant everything to everybody. Saying "no" is as important as granting things, especially among those in command. What matters is the way you do it. Some people's "no" is prized more highly than the "yes" of others: a gilded "no" pleases more than a curt "yes." Many people always have "no" on their lips, and they sour everything. "No" is what occurs to them first. They may give in later, but they aren't well thought of because they started out by being so unpleasant. Refusal shouldn't come in one fell blow. Let people nibble on their disappointment little by little. Never refuse something completely: others would no longer depend on you. There should always be some last remnants of hope to sweeten the bitterness of refusal. Let courtesy occupy the void where favor once stood, and good words compensate for a lack of action. "No" and "yes" are short words requiring long thought.

71 *Don't be inconsistent, either because of temperament or out of affectation.* The prudent man is consistent in all things pertaining to perfection, and this speaks well for his intelligence. Only the causes and relative merits of things can change his behavior.

When it comes to prudence, variety is ugly. There are some people who are different each day. Their luck changes daily, and so do their will and their powers of understanding. Yesterday they conceded; today they receded. They belie their own reputation, confusing others.

72 *Be resolute.* Faulty execution does less harm than a lack of resolution. Materials turn bad more often in repose than in motion. There are people who can't make up their minds and need a push from others. At times this is caused not by perplexity, for they see clearly enough, but by inactivity. It may be ingenious to identify difficulties, but it is more so to find a way of eluding them. Other people are bogged down by nothing and have great powers of judgment and resolution. They were born for lofty pursuits and their clear understanding lets them succeed with ease. No sooner done than said, and there is still time left over. Sure of their luck, they venture forth with even greater confidence.

73 *Know when to be evasive.* It is the way the prudent get out of difficulty. With an elegant joke they are able to escape from the most intricate laby-

rinth. One smile and they have eluded difficulty. On this the greatest of captains* founded his courage. A friendly way of saying no is to change the subject, and no ploy is more clever than to pretend it isn't you, but someone else, who is being alluded to.

74

Don't be unfriendly. The wildest animals inhabit cities. Being unapproachable is the vice of those who lack self-knowledge and who change humors with honors. To begin by annoying others is no way to win renown. Imagine one of these surly monsters, always about to turn savage and impertinent. His unlucky servants approach him as though he were a tiger, arming themselves cautiously with a whip. In order to reach their high position they pleased everyone, and now that they are there they want to get even by angering everyone. Because of their position, such people ought to belong to everyone, but their harshness and vanity makes them belong to no one. A courtly punishment for them: avoid them entirely. Bestow your wisdom on others.

---

*Gonzalo de Córdoba, "El Gran Capitán" (the Great Captain), military man known for his exploits in the war against the Moors and in southern Italy.

75 *Choose a heroic model*, and emulate rather than imitate. There are examples of greatness, living texts of renown. Let each person choose the first in his field, not so much to follow him as to surpass them. Alexander cried at the tomb of Achilles, not for Achilles but for himself, for unlike Achilles, he had not yet been born to fame.* Nothing makes the spirit so ambitious as the trumpet of someone else's fame. It frightens away envy and encourages noble deeds.

76 *Don't always be joking.* Prudence is known for its seriousness, which wins more respect than wit. The person who is always joking falls laughably short of perfection. We treat him like a liar, never believing him. From one we fear deceit, from the other jest. One never knows when jokers are exercising their judgment, which is the same as not having any. No humor is worse than continual humor. Some win a reputation for wit, and lose their wits. There are moments for joviality, but the rest of the time belongs to seriousness.

*According to Plutarch, Alexander the Great cried enviously before the tomb of Achilles because the latter had been lucky enough to be immortalized by Homer.

77 *Adapt yourself to everyone else.* A Proteus of discretion. Learned with the learned, saintly with saints. This is a great way to capture the goodwill of others, for similarity generates benevolence. Observe people's temperaments, and adapt yourself accordingly. Whether you're with a serious person or a jovial one, follow the current, and politely transform yourself. This is especially true of those who depend on others. It is a great stratagem for living prudently, and it requires much capacity. It is less difficult for the person with a well-informed intellect and varied tastes.

78 *Skill at trying things out.* Folly always rushes into action, for all fools are bold. Their very simplicity, which prevents them from foreseeing danger, keeps them from worrying about their reputation. But Prudence enters with great care. Caution and Penetration precede her, beating the bushes so that she can advance safely. Discretion sentences hasty action to failure, though Fortune sometimes issues a pardon. Go slowly when you fear the depths. Let shrewdness feel its way forward and Prudence steer you toward firm ground. These days there are pitfalls in dealing with others, and it is best to fathom things as you go along.

79 *A jovial character.* In moderation, it is a gift, not a defect. A pinch of wit is good seasoning. The greatest people can parlay grace and humor into universal favor. But they pay due respect to prudence and never break with decorum. Others use jest as a quick way out of difficulty. Some things should be taken jokingly, even those that others take most seriously. This shows a certain agreeableness, and works like a strange charm on the hearts of others.

80 *Be careful when you inform yourself about things.* Much of our lives is spent gathering information. We see very few things for ourselves, and live trusting others. The ears are the back door of truth and the front door of deceit. Truth is more often seen than heard. Seldom does it reach us unalloyed, even less so when it comes from afar. It is always blended with the emotions it has passed through. Emotion taints everything it touches, making it odious or favorable. It tries always to impress us one way or another. Be more careful with someone who is praising than with someone who is criticizing. Discover what ax he is grinding, on what side he is limping, where he is heading. Beware of the false and the faulty.

81 *Renew your brilliance.* It is the privilege of the Phoenix. Excellence grows old and so does fame. Custom wears down our admiration, and a mediocre novelty can conquer the greatest eminence in its old age. So be reborn in courage, in intellect, in happiness, and in all else. Dare to renew your brilliance, dawning many times, like the sun, only changing your surroundings. Withhold it and make people miss it; renew it and make them applaud.

82 *Neither all bad nor all good.* A certain sage reduced the whole of wisdom to the golden mean. Carry right too far and it becomes wrong. The orange squeezed completely dry gives only bitterness. Even in enjoyment you shouldn't go to extremes. The intellect itself will go dry if pressed too hard, and if you milk a cow like a tyrant you will draw only blood.

83 *Allow yourself some venial fault.* An act of carelessness can sometimes be the best way to help others see your talents. Envy often ostracizes people: the more civil it is, the more criminal. It accuses what is very perfect of sinning by not sinning, and it

condemns complete perfection. It makes itself into an Argos, looking for the faults in excellent things, if only to console itself. Like lightning, censure strikes the highest places. So let Homer nod at times, and pretend that your intelligence or courage—though not your prudence—has committed some act of carelessness. That way malevolence will calm down, and not burst its bubble of poison. This is like waving a red cape in front of the bull of envy in order to escape with immortality.

84 *Know how to use your enemies.* Grasp things not by the blade, which will harm you, but by the hilt, which will defend you. The same applies to emulation. The wise person finds enemies more useful than the fool does friends. Malevolence often levels the mountains of difficulty that favor made fearful. Many owe their greatness to their enemies. Flattery is fiercer than hatred, for hatred corrects the faults flattery had disguised. The prudent man makes a mirror out of the evil eye of others, and it is more truthful than that of affection, and helps him reduce his defects or emend them. One grows very cautious when living across the border from malevolent rivals.

85 *Don't be the wild card.** Excellent things are easily abused. When everyone covets something, they are easily annoyed by it. It is a bad thing to be good for nothing, but worse to be good for everything. Some lose because they win so often, and soon they are as despised as they once were desired. Such wild cards are found in every sort of perfection. They lose their initial reputation for uniqueness, and are scorned as common. The remedy for extremes is not to exceed the golden mean in displaying your gifts. Be excessive in your perfection but moderate about showing it. The brighter the torch, the more it consumes itself and the less it lasts. To win true esteem, make yourself scarce.

86 *Head off rumor.* The crowd is a many-headed monster: many eyes for malice, many tongues for slander. Sometimes a rumor arises and blights the best reputation, and if it sticks to you like a nickname, your fame will perish. The crowd usually seizes on some outstanding weakness, or some ridiculous defect: fit material for its murmurings. At times it is

*The wild card or joker: the one that can be anything its holder pleases.

our envious rivals who cunningly invent these defects. There are mean mouths and they ruin a great reputation sooner with a joke than with a shameless bold-faced lie. It is very easy to acquire a bad reputation, for badness is easily believed and hard to erase. Let the prudent person avoid all this, and keep an eye on vulgar insolence; for an ounce of prevention is worth a pound of cure.

87 *Culture and refinement.* Man is born a barbarian. Culture raises him above the beast. Culture turns us into true persons: the more culture, the greater the person. In that belief, Greece called the rest of the universe "barbarian." Ignorance is rough and rude. There is nothing more cultivating than knowledge. But wisdom herself is coarse when polish is lacking. Not only must understanding be refined, but also our desires and especially our conversation. Some people show a natural refinement both in their inner and outer gifts, their concepts and words, in their bodily adornment (which is like the bark) and their spiritual gifts (the fruit). Others are so gross that they tarnish everything, even their fine qualities, with an unbearable barbaric sloppiness.

88 *Deal with others in a grand way.* Aspire to elevation. The great should never be petty. You needn't go into all the details when conversing with others, especially when the subject is distasteful. Notice things, but do so casually; it isn't good to turn conversation into detailed interrogation. Act with a courteous, noble generality, which is a sort of gallantry. A large part of ruling lies in feigning indifference. Learn to overlook most of the things that happen among your close friends, your acquaintances, and especially your enemies. Overscrupulousness is irritating, and if it forms part of your character you will be tiresome to others. To keep circling around something unpleasant is a sort of mania. Remember that people usually behave like what they are: according to their own heart and their own capacity.

89 *Know yourself:* your character, intellect, judgment, and emotions. You cannot master yourself if you do not understand yourself. There are mirrors for the face, but the only mirror for the spirit is wise self-reflection. And when you stop caring about your outer image, try to emend and improve the inner one. In order to undertake matters wisely, gauge your

prudence and perspicacity. Judge how well you measure up to a challenge. Plumb your depths, weigh your resources.

90 *The art of living long: live well.* Two things bring life to an early end: stupidity and depravity. Some lose their life by not knowing how to save it; others, by not wanting to. Just as virtue is its own reward, vice is its own punishment. The person who races through a life of vice comes to a doubly quick end. The one who races through virtue never dies. The strength of the mind is communicated to the body. A good life is long both in intention and extension.

91 *Never act unless you think it prudent to do so.* If the person doing something suspects he will fail, it will be evident to the person watching, even more so when he is a rival. If your judgment wavers in the heat of emotion, you'll be thought a fool when things cool down. It is dangerous to undertake something when you doubt its wisdom. It would be safer not to act at all. Prudence refuses to deal in probability: it always walks under the midday sun of reason. How can something turn out well when caution started to condemn it the moment it was conceived? Even resolutions that passed the inner examination *nemine discrepante** often turn out badly; so what can we expect from those that reason doubted over and judgment considered rash?

92

Transcendent wisdom, in every situation. This is the first and highest rule in acting and speaking, the more necessary the greater and higher your occupation. An ounce of prudence is worth a pound of cleverness. It's more a matter of walking surely than of courting vulgar applause. A reputation for prudence is the ultimate triumph of fame. It is enough if you satisfy the prudent, whose approval is the touchstone of success.

93

A universal man. Possessing every perfection, he is equal to many men. He makes life ever so pleasant, communicating that enjoyment to his friends. Variety and perfection are what makes life delightful. It is a great art to know how to enjoy all good things. And since Nature made man a compen-

*With no one dissenting.

dium of the whole natural world, let art make him a universe by training his taste and intellect.

94 *Unfathomable gifts.* The prudent person—if he wants to be revered by others—should never allow them to judge the extent of his knowledge and courage. Allow yourself to be known, but not comprehended. No one will discern the limits of your talent, and thus no one will be disappointed. You can win more admiration by keeping other people guessing the extent of your talent, or even doubting it, than you can by displaying it, however great.

95 *Keep expectations alive.* Keep nourishing them. Let much promise more, and let great deeds make people expect still greater ones. Don't show everything you have on the first roll of the dice. The trick is to moderate your strength and knowledge and advance little by little toward success.

96 *Good common sense.* It is the throne of reason, the foundation of prudence, and by its light it is easy to succeed. It is a gift from heaven, highly prized

because it is first and best. Good sense is our armor, so necessary that the lack of this single piece will make people call us lacking. When least present, most missed. All actions in life depend on its influence, and all solicit its approval, for all depends on intelligence. It consists of a natural inclination to all that conforms most to reason, and to all that is most fit.

97 *Make your reputation and keep it.* We enjoy it on loan from Fame. It is expensive, for it is born from eminence, which is as rare as mediocrity is common. Once attained, it is easily kept. It confers many an obligation, performs many a deed. It is a sort of majesty when it turns into veneration, through the sublimity of its origin and sphere of action. Reputations based on substance are the ones that have always endured.

98 *Write your intentions in cipher.* The passions are the gates of the spirit. The most practical sort of knowledge lies in dissimulation. The person who shows his cards risks losing. Let caution and reserve combat the attentiveness of others. When your opponent sees into your reasoning like a lynx, conceal your thoughts like an inky cuttlefish. Let no one discover

your inclinations, no one foresee them, either to contradict or to flatter them.

99   *Reality and appearance.* Things pass for
what they seem, not for what they are. Only rarely
do people look into them, and many are satisfied with
appearances. It isn't enough to be right if your face
looks malicious and wrong.

100   *A man free of deceit and illusion*, one
who is virtuous and wise, a courtly philosopher. But
do not be so only in appearance, or flaunt your virtue.
Philosophy is no longer revered, although it is the
chief pursuit of the wise. The science of prudence is
no longer venerated. Seneca introduced it to Rome,
and for a time it appealed to the noble. But now it is
considered useless and bothersome. And yet freeing
oneself from deceit has always been food for prudence,
and one of the delights of righteousness.

101   *Half the world is laughing at the other
half, and folly rules over all.* Either everything is good
or everything is bad, depending on how you look at

it. What one person pursues, another shuns. It is an insufferable fool who measures all things by his own opinion. Perfection does not mean pleasing one person alone: tastes are as abundant as faces and just as varied. There is no defect that someone does not value, and you need not lower your opinion because a thing doesn't please some people: there will be others to appreciate it, and their applause, in turn, will be condemned. The norm of true satisfaction is the approval of renowned people who know how to judge each class of things. One does not live by following one opinion, one custom, or one century.

102

A stomach for big helpings of fortune. The body of Prudence should have a big gullet. A great talent is made up of great parts. If you deserve the best luck, don't eat your fill of *good* luck. What is surfeit to some is hunger to others. Some people waste exquisite food because they have no stomach for it: they weren't born for, and aren't accustomed to, high occupations. Their relations with others turn to vinegar, and a false sense of honor clouds their head and makes them lose it. They grow dizzy in high places, and are beside themselves because there is no room in them for luck. Let the great person show that he still has room for better things, and carefully avoid all that would show a narrow heart.

103 *To each, the dignity that befits him.* Not everyone is a king, but your deeds should be worthy of one, within the limits of your class and condition. A regal way of doing things. Sublimity of action, a lofty mind. You should resemble a king in merit, if not in reality, for true sovereignty lies in integrity. You won't envy greatness if you yourself can be a norm of greatness. Especially those who are near the throne should acquire something of true superiority. They should share the moral gifts of majesty rather than the pomp, and aspire to things lofty and substantial rather than to imperfect vanity.

104 *Have a good sense of what each job requires.* Jobs vary and it takes knowledge and discernment to understand that variety. Some jobs take courage, others subtlety. The easiest ones are those that depend on honesty; the most difficult, those that require artifice. The former require only natural talent; the latter, all sorts of attentiveness and vigilance. It is much work to govern men, and even more, fools or madmen. It takes double intelligence to rule those who have none. The job that is unbearable is the one that takes over the whole person, working full-time, always in the same manner. Far better are

the jobs we don't grow bored with, where variety combines with importance and refreshes our taste. The jobs most respected are the ones that entail the most, or least, dependence. And the worst are those that make us sweat the hardest, both here and (even harder) in the hereafter.

105 *Don't be tiresome.* Don't have only one theme, one obsession. Brevity is pleasant and flattering, and it gets more done. It gains in courtesy what it loses in curtness. Good things, if brief: twice good. Badness, if short, isn't so bad. Quintessences work better than farragoes. Everyone knows that a tall person is rarely an intelligent one, but it's better to be tall in stature than long in conversation. Some people are better at disturbing than adorning the universe: useless trinkets shunned by all. The discreet person should avoid tiring others, especially the great, who are very busy. It would be worse to irritate one of them than the rest of the world. Well said is quickly said.

106 *Don't flaunt your good fortune.* It is more offensive to take excessive pride in your high office

than in yourself. Don't play the "great man"—it is odious—and don't be proud of being envied. The more strenuously you seek esteem from others, the less of it you will have. It depends on respect. You can't simply grab it, you have to deserve it and wait for it. Important occupations call for a certain gravity and decorum. Keep only what the occupation requires, what you need to fulfill your obligations. Don't squeeze it dry; help it along. Those who want to look like hard workers give the impression that they aren't up to their jobs. If you want to succeed, do so using your gifts, not your outer trappings. Even a king ought to be venerated more because of his person than because of his pomp and circumstance.

107 *Don't look self-satisfied.* Don't go through life feeling discontent with yourself, which is timidity, or satisfied, which is foolishness. Self-complacency usually arises from ignorance, and it leads to a foolish happiness that tickles the taste but ruins the reputation. Unable to discern the high perfection of others, it is content with its own vulgar mediocrity. Caution is always useful, either to help things turn out well or to console us when they turn out badly. No setback will surprise you if you fear it beforehand. Homer himself nodded at times, and

Alexander tumbled from his estate and from the deceit in which he was living. Things depend on circumstance. Sometimes they prevail, and sometimes fail. For a hopeless fool, however, the emptiest satisfaction turns into a flower that goes on scattering its seed.

108 *A shortcut to becoming a true person*: put the right people beside you. The company you keep can work wonders. Customs and tastes and even intelligence are transmitted without our being aware of it. Let the quick person join the hesitant one, and so on, through every sort of temperament. That way you will achieve moderation without straining after it. It takes much skill to know how to adapt yourself. The alternation of opposites makes the universe beautiful and sustains it, and causes even greater harmony in human customs than in nature. Govern yourself by this advice when you select your friends and servants. The communication of extremes will produce a discreet and golden mean.

109 *Don't berate others*. There are people with savage tempers who make everything a crime, not out of passion but because of their very character. They condemn everyone, some for what they've done, others for what they will do. This shows a spirit worse than cruel, which is truly vile. They criticize others so exaggeratedly that they make motes into beams in order to poke out eyes. They are taskmasters who can turn a paradise into a prison. When swayed by passion, they take everything to extremes. Good-natured people are able to pardon anything. They insist that others had good intentions or went wrong inadvertently.

110 *Don't wait to be a setting sun.* It is a maxim of prudent people to abandon things before being abandoned by them. You should make even your end into a triumph. At times the sun itself retires behind a cloud so that no one will see it fall, and it leaves us wondering whether it has set or not. Avoid sunsets so as not to burst with misfortune. Don't wait for people to turn their shoulders on you: they will bury you alive to your regret, dead to renown. The prudent know when to retire a racehorse, and do not wait for him to collapse in the middle of the race, to the laughter of all. Let Beauty shatter the mirror cleverly, at the right time, and not too late when she cannot bear the truth.

111 *Have friends.* They are a second being. To a friend, all friends are good and wise. When you are with them, all turns out well. You are worth as much as others want you to be and say you are, and the way to their mouths lies through their hearts. Nothing bewitches like service to others, and the best way to win friends is to act like one. The most and best we have depends on others. You must live either with friends or with enemies. Win one each day, if not as a confidant, at least as a follower. Choose well and some will remain whom you can trust.

112 *Win the goodwill of others.* Even the first and highest Cause,* in the most important matters, does things this way. Reputation is purchased with affection. Some trust so much in their own worth that they make light of diligence. But the prudent person knows very well that merit can take a shortcut if helped by favor. Benevolence makes everything easier and compensates for whatever is lacking: courage, integrity, wisdom, and even discretion. It never sees ugliness, for it doesn't want to. It is usually born from similarity of temperament, race, family,

*The divinity.

country, or occupation. In the spiritual realm, benevolence bestows talent, favor, reputation, and merit. Once one wins it—and this is difficult—it is easily kept. You can make an effort to win it, but you must also know how to use it.

113

Plan for bad fortune while your fortune is good. In the summer it is wise to provide for winter, and it is easier to do so. Favors are less expensive, and friendships abound. It is good to save up for a rainy day: adversity is expensive and all is lacking. Keep a following of friends and grateful people; someday you will value what now seems unimportant. Villainy has no friends in prosperity because it refuses to recognize them. In adversity it is the other way around.

114

Never compete. When you vie with your opponents, your reputation suffers. Your competitor will immediately try to find your faults and discredit you. Few wage war fairly. Rivalry discovers the defects that courtesy overlooks. Many people had a good reputation until they acquired rivals. The heat of opposition revives dead infamies and digs up the stench of the past. Competition begins by revealing faults and rivals take advantage of everything they can and all they ought not to. Often they gain nothing by offending others, only the vile satisfaction of revenge. Revenge blows the dust of oblivion from people's faults. Benevolence was always peaceable, and reputation indulgent.

115 *Get used to the failings of your friends, family, and acquaintances*, as you do to ugly faces. Where there is dependence, try for convenience. There are nasty-minded people whom we cannot live with and cannot live without. It takes skill to get used to them, as we do to ugliness, so that they won't surprise us on some dire occasion. At first they frighten us, but little by little they stop looking so horrible, and caution foresees, or learns to tolerate, their unpleasantness.

116 *Always deal with people of principle.* Favor them and win their favor. Their very rectitude ensures they will treat you well even when they oppose you, for they act like who they are, and it is better to fight with good-minded people than to conquer the

bad. There is no way to get along with villainy, for it feels no obligation to behave rightly. This is why there is no true friendship among villains, and their fine words cannot be trusted; for they do not spring from honor. Avoid the person who has no honor, for if he esteems not honor, he esteems not virtue. And honor is the throne of integrity.

117 *Don't talk about yourself.* You must either praise yourself, which is vanity, or criticize yourself, which is meekness. You show a lack of good judgment and become a nuisance to others. If this is important among friends, it is even more so in high positions, where one often speaks in public and where any appearance of vanity passes for foolishness. Nor is it prudent to talk about people who are present. You risk running aground on flattery or vituperation.

118 *Be known for your courtesy*: it alone can make you worthy of praise. Courtesy is the best part of culture, a kind of enchantment, and it wins the goodwill of all, just as rudeness wins only scorn and universal annoyance. When rudeness comes from pride, it is detestable; when from bad breeding, it is

contemptible. Better too much courtesy than too little, or the same sort for everyone, for that would lead to injustice. Treat your enemies with courtesy, and you'll see how valuable it really is. It costs little but pays a nice dividend: those who honor are honored. Politeness and a sense of honor have this advantage: we bestow them on others without losing a thing.

119 *Don't make yourself disliked.* There is no need to provoke aversion, it comes without being called. There are many who hate for no particular reason, without knowing how or why. Malevolence travels much faster than the desire to please. A desire for vengeance will harm you more quickly and surely than a desire for material goods. Some want to be disliked by all, either because they want to cause annoyance or because they feel it. Once hatred takes command of them, it is as hard to get rid of as a bad reputation. These people fear men of judgment, despise those who speak ill, disdain the arrogant, abominate buffoons, but they spare people of singular excellence. Show your esteem if you want to be esteemed, and if you want to be rewarded with success, reward others with your attention.

120 *Live practically.* Even your knowledge should seem usual and usable, and where knowledge is uncommon, feign ignorance. Ways of thinking change, and so does taste. Don't think like an ancient; taste like a modern. Count heads. That is what matters in all things. When you must, follow the common taste, and make your way toward eminence. The wise should adapt themselves to the present, even when the past seems more attractive, both in the clothes of the soul and in those of the body. This rule for living holds for everything but goodness, for one must always practice virtue. Many things have come to seem old-fashioned: speaking truth, keeping your word. Good people seem to belong to the good old days, though they are always beloved. If any exist, they are rare, and they are never imitated. What a sad age this is, when virtue is rare and malice is common. The prudent must live as best they can, though not as they would like to. May they prefer what luck granted them to what it withheld!

121 *Don't make much ado about nothing.* Some take nothing into account, and others want to account for everything. They are always talking

importance, always taking things too seriously, turning them into debate and mystery. Few bothersome things are important enough to bother with. It is folly to take to heart what you should turn your back on. Many things that were something are nothing if left alone, and others that were nothing turn into much because we pay attention to them. In the beginning it is easy to put an end to problems, but not later. Sometimes the cure causes the disease. Not the least of life's rules is to leave well enough alone.

122 *Mastery in words and deeds.* It makes way everywhere, and quickly wins respect. It influences everything: conversation, making a speech, and even walking and looking and wanting. It is a great victory to seize the hearts of others. This sort of authority doesn't originate in foolish audacity or irritating slow-moving gravity; it is born from a superior character abetted by merit.

123 *A person without affectation.* The more talent, the less affectation. This is a truly vulgar blemish, as annoying to others as it is burdensome. It makes one a martyr to worry, for it is a torment to

have to keep up appearances. Even great gifts seem less valuable on account of affectation, for people attribute them to strain and artifice rather than to natural grace, and the natural is always more pleasant than the artificial. The affected are held as strangers to the talents they affect. The better you are at something, the more you should hide your efforts, so that perfection seems to occur naturally. Nor should you flee affectation by affecting not to have it. The prudent man should never acknowledge his own merits. By appearing to overlook them, he will gain the attention of others. The eminent person who takes no notice of his own perfection is twice eminent. He follows his own peculiar path to applause.

124 *Make yourself wanted.* Few have won popular favor; consider yourself fortunate if you can win the favor of the wise. People are usually lukewarm towards those at the end of their careers. There are ways to win and keep the grand prize of favor. You can be outstanding in your occupation and in your talents. A pleasant manner works too. Turn eminence into dependence, so that people will say that the occupation needed you, and not vice versa. Some people honor their position, others are honored by it. It is no honor to be made good by the bad person who

succeeds you. The fact that someone else is hated doesn't mean that you are truly wanted.

125 *Don't be a blacklist of others' faults.* To pay attention to the infamy of others shows that your own fame is ruined. Some would like to dissimulate, or cleanse, their own blemishes with those of others, or to console themselves with them: a consolation of fools. Their breath stinks; they are cesspools of filth. In these matters, he who digs deepest gets muddiest. Few escape some fault of their own, either by inheritance or by association. Only when you are little known are your faults unknown. The prudent person doesn't register the defects of others or become a vile, living blacklist.

126 *The fool isn't someone who does something foolish, but the one who doesn't know how to conceal it.* Hide your affects, but even more, your defects. All people err, but with this difference: the wise dissimulate their errors, and fools speak of those they are about to commit. Reputation is more a matter of stealth than of deeds. If you can't be chaste, be chary. The slips of the great are closely observed, like eclipses of the sun and moon. You shouldn't confide

your defects to friends, or even to yourself, were that possible. Another rule for living is applicable here: know how to forget.

127 *Ease and grace* in everything.* It gives life to talent, breath to speech, soul to deeds, and it sets off the highest gifts. The other perfections are an adornment of nature, but grace adorns the perfections themselves: it makes even thought more admirable. It owes most to natural privilege and least to effort, and it is superior even to the precepts of art. It runs faster than mere skill and overtakes even what is dashing. It increases self-confidence and heaps up perfection. Without it, all beauty is dead, all grace is disgrace. It transcends merit, discretion, prudence, and majesty itself. It is a seemly shortcut to getting things done, and a refined way to escape from any difficulty.

128 *Highmindedness.* It is one of the chief requisites of heroism, for it inspires all sorts of great-

---

*Despejo, rendered here as "ease and grace," might also be translated as "ineffable charm" or "charisma." Gracián's French translator rendered it as "le je-ne-sais-quoi."

ness. It heightens our taste, swells the heart, lifts up our thought, ennobles our condition, and allows majesty to do anything it wants. It stands out wherever it is found. Luck sometimes envies it and tries to deny it, but it yearns to excel. It rules the will, even when circumstances restrict it. Magnanimity, generosity, and all other eminent qualities acknowledge it as their source.

129 *Never complain.* Complaints will always discredit you. Rather than compassion and consolation, they provoke passion and insolence, and encourage those who hear our complaints to behave like those we complain about. Once divulged to others, the offenses done to us seem to make others pardonable. Some complain of past offenses and give rise to future ones. They want to be helped or consoled, but their listeners feel only satisfaction and even contempt. It is better policy to praise the favors others have done you, so as to win still more of them. When you tell how those absent have favored you, you are asking those present to do the same, and pay in the same coin. The prudent person should never publicize dishonor or slights, only the esteem others have shown him. Thus will he have friends and halve his enemies.

130 *Do, but also seem.* Things do not pass for what they are, but for what they seem. To excel and to know how to show it is to excel twice. What is invisible might as well not exist. Reason itself is not venerated when it does not wear a reasonable face. Those easily duped outnumber the prudent. Deceit reigns, and things are judged from without, and are seldom what they seem. A fine exterior is the best recommendation of inner perfection.

131 *A gallant spirit.* The soul has its fine dress clothes, the spiritual dash and boldness that make the heart look splendid. Not everyone has room for gallantry, for it calls for magnanimity. Its first concern is always to speak well of the enemy, and act even better. It shines most brightly when it has the chance to avenge itself. It does not avoid these situations, but takes advantage of them, turning a potential act of vengeance into an unexpected act of generosity. It is also the best part of governing others, the adornment of politics. It never shows off its triumphs—it affects nothing—and when they are due to merit, it knows how to dissimulate.

132 *Reconsider.* Safety lies in looking things over twice, especially when you are not completely confident. Take time, either to concede something or to better your situation, and you will find new ways to confirm and corroborate your judgment. If it is a matter of giving, a gift is valued more highly when bestowed wisely than when given quickly. What was long desired is always more appreciated. If it is a matter of refusing, you can devote more attention to your manner, and let your "no" ripen a bit, so that it will not be quite so bitter. Most of the time, the first heat of desire will have died down, and it will be easier to accept refusal. If someone asks soon, grant late. This is a way of holding his interest.

133 *Better to be mad with everyone than sane all alone*: so say the politicians. If all are mad, you'll be equal to them. And if you alone are sane, you will be taken for mad. What matters is to follow the current. The best knowledge, sometimes, is not to know, or pretend not to. We must live with others, and the majority are ignorant. To live by yourself, you must be very godly or a complete savage. But I would modify this aphorism and say: Better sane with

the many than mad all by yourself. Some people want to be singular in the pursuit of chimeras.

134 *Double your store of life's necessities*. You will double life. Don't depend on any single thing, or limit any one resource, no matter how rare and excellent. Double everything, especially the sources of benefit, favor, and taste. The moon is transcendently mutable, setting the limits of permanence, and more mutable still are the things that depend on our frail human will. Store up supplies for frailty. It is a great rule for living to double your sources of happiness and profit. Just as nature doubled the most important and most exposed of our bodily limbs, so should art double the things we depend on.

135 *Don't have the spirit of contradiction*. You will only burden yourself with foolishness and annoyance. Let prudence plot against it. Finding objections to everything can be ingenious, but the stubborn person is almost always a fool. Some turn sweet conversation into a skirmish, and are more of an enemy to their friends and acquaintances than to those with whom they have no dealings. The bone of

contention is hardest when the morsel is sweetest, and contradiction often ruins happy moments. They are pernicious fools who add nastiness to beastliness.

136 *Size up the matter.* Take the pulse of the business at hand. Many see the trees but not the forest, or bark up the wrong tree, speaking endlessly, reasoning uselessly, without going to the pith of the matter. They go round and round, tiring themselves and us, and never get to what is important. This happens to people with confused minds who do not know how to clear away the brambles. They waste time and patience on what it would be better to leave alone, and later there is no time for what they left.

137 *The wise are sufficient unto themselves.* One of them carried all of his belongings with him.* One friend—a universal man—can represent Rome and the rest of the universe.** Be that friend to your-

---

*The Greek philosopher Stilpon of Megara, having lost his wife, his children, and all of his possessions in a fire, emerged from the ruins and remarked: "I have all my possessions with me." Romera-Navarro observes that Gracián had read of this in one of Seneca's *Moral Epistles*.

**An allusion to Cato the Elder, statesman and soldier, praised by Cicero for his capacity for friendship.

self, and you will be able to live by yourself. Why should you need anyone else if no taste and no understanding is superior to yours? You will depend only on yourself; the greatest happiness is to resemble the Supreme Entity. The person who can live by himself is in no way a brute; in many ways he is a wise man, in every way a god.

138 *Leave things alone.* Especially when the sea—people, your friends, your acquaintances—is stirred up. Life with others has its tempests, its storms of will, when it is wise to retire to a safe harbor and let the waves subside. Remedies often worsen evils. Let nature take its course, and morality. The wise physician knows when to prescribe and when not to, and sometimes it takes skill not to apply remedies. Throwing up your hands is sometimes a good way to put down vulgar storms. If you bow to time for the present, you will conquer in the future. It takes little to muddy a stream. You can't make it grow clear by trying to, only by leaving it alone. There is no better remedy for disorder than to leave it alone to correct itself.

139 *Know your unlucky days*, for they exist. Nothing will turn out right. You can change your game, but bad luck will remain. Test your luck a few times, and retire if it is bad. Even understanding has its moments: no one can know everything at all hours. It takes good luck to think well, as it does to write a good letter. All perfection depends upon the right moment. Even beauty isn't always in season. Discretion goes into hiding, either doing too much or too little. To turn out well, everything has its moment. On some days, everything goes badly; on others, well, and with less effort. You find that everything is done easily, your intelligence is in working order, your temperament in tune, and you are your own lucky star. Take advantage of such days, and don't waste a moment of them. But it isn't smart to pronounce the day definitively bad because of one bad stroke of luck, or do the contrary.

140

Go straight to the good in everything. It is the happy lot of those with good taste. The bee goes straight for sweetness, and the viper for the bitterness it needs for its poison. So with tastes: some go for the best, others for the worst. There is nothing that doesn't have something good, especially books, where good is imagined. Some people's temperaments are so unfortunate that among a thousand perfections they will find a single defect and censure it and blow it out of proportion. They are the garbage collectors of the will and of the intellect, burdened down with blemishes and defects: punishment for their poor discernment rather than proof of their subtlety. They are unhappy, for they batten on bitterness and graze on imperfections. Others have a happier sort of taste: among a thousand defects they discover some perfection that good luck happened to let drop.

141 *Don't listen to yourself.* What good is it to please yourself if you don't please others? Self-satisfaction reaps only scorn. By giving yourself credit, you will run up a debt with others. Speaking and listening to yourself is impossible to do well. To speak to yourself is madness; to listen to yourself in front of others, doubly mad. Some people batter our ears with refrains like "Am I right?" or "You know?", badgering others for approbation or flattery, and casting doubt on their own judgment. Vain people, too, like to speak with an echo. They put their conversation on high heels, and fools rush to their rescue with an odious "Well said!"

142 *Don't defend the wrong side out of stubbornness,* just because your opponent happened to get there first and choose the best. You will go into battle

already defeated, and go down in disgrace. Bad is no match for good. It was cunning of your opponent to anticipate the best, and it would be stupid of you to defend the worst. Those obstinate in deeds are in greater danger than those obstinate in words, for there is greater risk in doing than in saying. The vulgar ignorance of stubborn people makes them prefer contradiction to truth and contention to utility. Prudent people are on the side of reason, not passion, whether because they foresaw it from the first, or because they improved their position later. If your opponent is a fool, his foolishness will make him change course, switch sides, and worsen his position. To expel him from the best, embrace it yourself. His foolishness will make him abandon it and his own obstinacy will cast him down.

143 *Don't be paradoxical to avoid being vulgar.* Both extremes bring discredit. Anything that threatens our dignity is a kind of foolishness. The paradox is a sort of deceit that seems plausible at first and startles us with its piquant novelty. But later, when its falseness is revealed, it brings disgrace. It possesses a certain false charm, and in politics it can be the ruin of states. Those who cannot distinguish themselves through virtue take the path of paradox, surprising fools and turning wise men into prophets.

Paradox reveals an unsound judgment and a lack of prudence. It is based on falsity or uncertainty, and puts dignity at risk.

144

Enter conceding and come out winning. This is a strategy for getting what you want. Even in heavenly matters, our Christian teachers recommend this holy craftiness. It is an important sort of dissimulation and you use it to capture someone else's will. You appear to have his interests in mind, but it is only to open the way for yours. You should never take up matters confusedly, especially risky ones. Be careful with people whose first word is usually "no." It is best to disguise your intent, so that they won't realize the difficulties of saying "yes," especially when you have already sensed their resistance. This maxim relates to the ones about hidden intentions, and requires the same quintessential subtlety.

145

Hide your wounded finger, or you will bump it on everything. Never complain about it. Malice always zeroes in on what hurts or weakens us. Look discouraged and you will only encourage others to make fun of you. Evil intent is always looking for ways to get a rise out of you. It uses insinuation to discover where you hurt, and knows a thousand stratagems to probe your wounds. If you are wise, you will ignore malicious hints, and conceal your troubles, either personal or inherited, for even Fortune sometimes likes to hit you where it hurts. It always goes straight for raw flesh. Be careful not to reveal what mortifies and what vivifies you, lest the former last and the latter end.

146 *Look deep inside.* Things are seldom what they seem, and ignorance, which sees no deeper than the bark, often turns to disillusion when it penetrates into things. In all things, deceit arrives first, dragging fools behind it in endless vulgarity. Truth is always late, always last to arrive, limping along with Time. Prudent people save one of their ears for truth, thanking their common mother, Nature, for giving them two. Deceit is superficial, and superficial people are quick to run into her. Discernment lives hidden away in retirement, so as to be more esteemed by the wise and the discreet.

147 *Don't be inaccessible.* No one is so perfect as not to need occasional counsel. The person

who doesn't listen is a hopeless fool. Even the most independent of people ought to heed friendly advice, and even sovereigns are happy to learn from others. Some people are incorrigible because inaccessible, and they fall because no one dares to catch them. Even the most inflexible person should leave the door open to friendship; help will come through it. We all need a friend who feels free to scold us and give us advice. Trust will grant him this authority, and our high opinion of his loyalty and prudence. We shouldn't bestow our respect and authority on just anyone, and yet, in the inner rooms of our caution, we need the faithful mirror of a confidant. If we value that mirror, it will set us free from deceit.

148 *Be skilled in conversation.* The art of conversation is the measure of a true person. No human activity calls for so much discretion, for none is more common. It is here that we win or lose. It takes prudence to write a letter, which is conversation thought out and written down, and even more to converse, for discretion is soon put to the test. Experts feel the tongue and quickly take the pulse of the mind. "Speak," said the sage, "and you will be known." To some the art of conversation lies in having no art at all, letting it fit loosely, like clothes. This may be

true of conversation among friends. In more elevated circles, conversation should be weightier, revealing the great substance of the person. To converse successfully, you must adapt yourself to the temperament and intelligence of others. Don't set yourself up as a censor of words—for you will be taken as a grammarian—and even less as a prosecutor of sentences —which will make others avoid you and keep you from communicating. In speech discretion matters more than eloquence.

149 *Let someone else take the hit.* You will shield yourself from malevolence: sound policy in those who govern. Having someone else take the blame for failure and be the butt of gossip does not spring from a lack of ability, as malice thinks, but from superior skill. Not everything can turn out well, and you can't please everyone. So look for a scapegoat, someone whose own ambition will make him a good target.

150 *Know how to sell your wares.* Intrinsic quality isn't enough. Not everyone bites at substance or looks for inner value. People like to follow the

crowd; they go someplace because they see other people do so. It takes much skill to explain something's value. You can use praise, for praise arouses desire. At other times you can give things a good name (but be sure to flee from affectation). Another trick is to offer something only to those in the know, for *everyone* believes himself an expert, and the person who isn't will want to be one. Never praise things for being easy or common: you'll make them seem vulgar and facile. Everybody goes for something unique. Uniqueness appeals both to the taste and to the intellect.

151 *Think ahead*: today for tomorrow— even many days ahead. The best providence is to have hours of it. To those forewarned, there are no strokes of bad luck; no tight spots for those who are prepared. Don't save your reason for difficult situations; use it to anticipate them. Difficult points require mature rethinking. The pillow is a tongueless sibyl, and it is better to sleep on something than to lie awake when things are on top of you. Some act, and think later: this is to look for excuses rather than consequences. Others think neither before nor after. Your whole life should be a matter of thinking out your destination. Rethinking and foresight are a good way to live in advance.

152 *Don't keep company with those who will make you seem less gifted*, either because they are superior or inferior. The more perfect someone is, the more highly he is esteemed. The other person will always play the leading role, and you a secondary one, and if you win any respect at all, it will come in scraps and remnants. When the moon is alone it competes with the stars, but once the sun comes out it either doesn't appear or it disappears. Don't go near the person who can eclipse you, only the one who will make you look better. This is how clever Fabula, from Martial's poem, was able to look beautiful and radiant among her ugly, unkempt maids. Don't have a pain in your side, or honor others to the detriment of your own reputation. To grow, associate with the eminent; once grown, with those who are average.

153 *Don't step into the huge gap left by some-one else.* If you do, be sure you have more than enough talent. Merely to equal your predecessor, you must be worth twice as much. It is a fine trick to make people prefer you to your successor, and it takes subtlety to avoid being eclipsed by your predecessor. To fill a great vacancy is hard, because the past always seems

better. It isn't enough to equal your predecessor; the person who goes first has an advantage. You need extra talent to expel him from his superior reputation.

154 *Neither quick to believe, nor quick to love.* A ripe judgment is slow to believe. Lying is ordinary; let belief be extraordinary. The rush to judgment leads to embarrassment and exhaustion. But don't cast doubt openly on the truthfulness of others. When you treat someone like a liar, or insist he has been deceived, you add insult to injury. There is an even greater disadvantage: not believing others implies that you yourself are deceitful. The liar suffers twice: he neither believes nor is believed. Prudent listeners suspend their judgment. Nor, an author tells us,* should we be quick to love. One lies with words, but also with things, and the latter sort of deceit results in more harm.

155 *Skill at mastering your passions.* Whenever possible, let reflection foresee the sudden movements of the passions. The prudent will do so easily. The first thing to do when you are upset is to notice

*Cicero.

that you *are*. You begin by mastering your emotions and determining not to go any further. With this superior sort of caution you can put a quick end to your anger. Know how to stop, and do so at the right moment: the most difficult thing about running is stopping. It speaks well for your judgment to remain lucid at moments of madness. Any excess of passion detracts from reason, but with this attentiveness, anger will never run away with you or trample on good sense. To get the best of an emotion, rein it in prudently. You will be the first sane man on horseback, and perhaps the last.*

156 *Select your friends.* They should be examined by discretion, tested by fortune, certified not only in willpower but also in understanding. Though success in life depends on this, people pay it little attention. In some cases, mere meddling leads to friendship and in most, mere chance. You are judged by the friends you have, and the wise never get along with fools. To take pleasure in someone's company doesn't make him a close friend. Sometimes we value his sense of humor without fully confiding in his talent. Some friendships are legitimate, others adulterous: the latter are for pleasure, the former are fertile

*"No one is wise on horseback," says the Spanish proverb.

and engender success. The insight of a friend is more valuable than the good wishes of many others. So let choice rule and not chance. Wise friends chase away sorrows, and foolish ones gather them. And don't wish your friends wealth if you want to keep them.

157 *Don't be mistaken about people*: it is the worst way to be deceived. Better to be cheated by the price than by the merchandise. There is nothing that requires more careful inspection. There is a difference between understanding things and knowing people, and it is a great art to penetrate temperaments and distinguish the humors of others. Human nature ought to be studied as closely as any book.

158 *Know how to use your friends*. It takes skill and discretion. Some are useful when near and others when far away, and the one who isn't good for conversation may be good for correspondence. Distance purifies certain defects that are unbearable at close range. You shouldn't seek only pleasure in your friends, but also utility. A friend is all things, and friendship has the three qualities of anything good: unity, goodness, and truth. Few people make good friends, and they are fewer still when we don't

know how to select them. Knowing how to keep a friend is more important than gaining a new one. Look for friends who can last, and when they're new, be satisfied that one day they will be old. The best ones of all are those well salted, with whom we have shared bushels of experience. Life without friends is a wasteland. Friendship multiplies good and shares evils. It is a unique remedy for bad luck and sweet relief to the soul.

159 *Know how to suffer fools.* The wise are the least tolerant, for learning has diminished their patience. Wide knowledge is hard to please. Epictetus tells us that the most important rule for living lies in knowing how to bear all things: to this he reduced half of wisdom. To tolerate foolishness much patience is needed. Sometimes we suffer most from those we most depend upon, and this helps us conquer ourselves. Patience leads to an inestimable inner peace, which is bliss on earth. And the person who does not know how to put up with others should retire into himself, if indeed he can suffer even himself.

160 *Speak prudently*: cautiously to your rivals, and with dignity to everyone else. There is always

time to utter a word, and never time to take it back. Speak as though you were writing your testament: the fewer words, the fewer lawsuits. Practice on what matters little for what matters much. Secrecy has the feel of divinity. The person quick to speak is no sooner greeted than defeated.

161 *Know your own sweet faults.* Even the most perfect person cannot escape them, but why marry them or take them as lovers? There are defects of the intellect and they are greatest—or noticed most easily—in people of great intelligence. Not because the person himself is not aware of them, but because he loves them. Two evils in one: irrational affection bestowed on faults. They are moles on the face of perfection. They repel others but to us they look like beauty marks. Here is a gallant way to conquer yourself, and add to your gifts. Others are quick to notice your faults. Instead of admiring your talent, they dwell on your defect, and use it to tarnish your other gifts.

162 *Conquer envy and malevolence.* It does little good to show indifference. Behave with gallantry and you will achieve much more. There is nothing

more praiseworthy than speaking well of someone who speaks badly of you; no vengeance more heroic than conquering and tormenting envy with merit and talent. Each of your successes will be torture for those who wish you ill, and your glory will be hell to your rivals. This is the greatest of punishments: to turn success into poison. The envious person dies not once, but as often as his rival lives in applause. Lasting fame for the envied means eternal punishment for the envious. The former lives forever in his glories, the latter in his punishment. The trumpets of fame play immortality for one and taps for the other, sentencing him to the gallows of anxiety.

163

Don't let your sympathy for the unfortunate make you one of them. What one man considers misfortune, another considers fortune. Who could call himself lucky if many others weren't? The unhappy often win people's sympathy; we want to compensate them, with useless favor, for the insults of fortune. The person whom everyone hated in prosperity is suddenly pitied by all. His downfall turns vengeance into compassion. It takes shrewdness to notice how the cards are being dealt. There are some people who associate only with the unfortunate. They pull up beside the unlucky soul whom they fled when he was fortunate. Sometimes this reveals an inner nobility, but it is anything but shrewd.

164

Float a trial balloon to see how well something is accepted and received, especially when you doubt its popularity or success. This assures you something will turn out well, and allows you to decide whether to move forward with it or withdraw it. By testing the will of others, the prudent person finds out where he stands. Maximum foresight in asking, wanting, and ruling.

165

Wage a clean war. The wise person can be driven to war, but not to a dishonorable one. Act like the person you are, not the way they make you act. To behave magnanimously towards your rivals is praiseworthy. You should fight not only to win power but also to show that you are a superior fighter. To conquer without nobility is not victory but surrender. The good man does not use forbidden weapons, like the ones he acquires when he breaks up with a friend. Even when friendship ends in hatred, don't take advantage of the trust that was once placed in you. Everything that smacks of treachery is poison to your reputation. Noble people shouldn't have even an atom of baseness. Nobility scorns villainy. You should be able to boast that if gallantry, generosity, and faith were lost in the world, they could be found again in your own breast.

166 *Distinguish the man of words from the man of deeds.* It is a subtle distinction, like the distinction between the friend who values you for yourself and the one who values your position. Bad words, even without bad deeds, are bad enough. But it is even worse, when you have no bad words, to have bad deeds. One cannot eat words (mere wind) or live on courtesy (polite deceit). To catch birds with mirrors is a perfect snare. Only the vain are satisfied with wind. To retain their worth, words must be backed up with deeds. Trees which give no fruit, only leaves, usually have no heart and pith. One must know which are profitable and which serve only for shade.

167 *Be self-reliant.* There is no better company, in tight situations, than a stout heart. When it is weak, use the organs closest to it. Worries are borne better by the self-reliant. Don't give in to fortune, or it will make itself even more unbearable. Some people help themselves little in their own travails, and double them by not knowing how to bear them. The person who knows himself overcomes his weakness with thoughtfulness, and the prudent manage to conquer all, even the stars.

168 *Don't become a monster of foolishness.* Among these monsters are all people who are vain, presumptuous, stubborn, whimsical, self-satisfied, extravagant, paradoxical, light-headed, seekers of novelty, the undisciplined . . . all are monsters of impertinence. Spiritual monstrosity is worse than bodily, for it contradicts a superior beauty. But who will correct all this common folly? Where good sense is lacking, there is no room for advice and direction. Careful observation has been pushed aside by an ill-conceived desire for imaginary applause.

169 *Better to avoid missing once than to hit the mark a hundred times.* No one looks directly at the sun, but everyone does when it is eclipsed. The vulgar will fasten upon your one failing rather than on your many successes. The bad are better known,

and attract more gossip, than the good. Many people were practically unknown until they sinned, and all their successes aren't enough to conceal a single tiny fault. Realize that malevolence will notice all your faults and none of your virtues.

170

In all matters, keep something in reserve. You'll preserve your usefulness. Don't use all your talents or deploy all your strength at all times. Even in knowledge hold something back: you will double your perfections. There must always be something you can use in a pinch. An opportune rescue is valued and honored more than a bold attack. Prudence always steers a safe course. In this sense also we can believe the piquant paradox: the half is much more than the whole.

171

Don't waste the favors people owe you. Keep important friends for great occasions. Don't spend their good graces and use your contacts for things that matter little. Keep your powder dry until you're really in danger. If you trade much for little, what will remain for later? There's nothing more precious than a favor or people to protect you. They can make or break anything: they can even give you wit, or take it away. Whatever nature and fame bestow on wise men, Fortune envies. It's even more important to hang on to people than to hang on to things.

172 *Never compete with someone who has nothing to lose.* The struggle will be unequal. One of the contestants enters the fray unencumbered, for he has already lost everything, even his shame. He has cast off everything, has nothing further to lose, and throws himself headlong into all sorts of insolence. Never risk your precious reputation on such a person. It took many years to win it, and it can be lost in a moment, on something far from momentous. One breath of scandal freezes much honorable sweat. The righteous person knows how much is at stake. He knows what can damage his reputation, and, because he commits himself prudently, he proceeds slowly, so that prudence has ample time to retreat. Not even if he triumphs will he win back what he lost by exposing himself to the risk of losing.

173 *Don't be made of glass in your dealings with others.* Even less so in friendship. Some people

break very easily, revealing how fragile they are. They fill up with resentment and fill others with annoyance. They are more sensitive than the pupils of the eyes, which cannot be touched, either in jest or in earnest. They take offense at motes: beams aren't even necessary. Those who deal with them must use great caution, and never forget their delicacy. The slightest slight annoys them. They are full of themselves, slaves to their own taste (for the sake of which they trample on everything else), and idolaters of their own silly sense of honor.

174 *Don't live in a hurry.* If you know how to organize things, you will know how to enjoy them. Many have life left over when luck runs out. They waste their happy moments and further down the road would like to turn around and return to them. Time moves too slowly for them, and, postilions of life, they spur it on with their own rash temperament. They want to devour in a day what they could hardly digest in a lifetime. They anticipate their successes, gulp down years of the future, and since they are always in a hurry, they soon finish everything. Even in the desire for knowledge you should show moderation so that things known won't be badly known. There are more days than luck. Be quick to act, slow

to enjoy. Deeds are good, and content is bad, when they are over.

175 *A person of substance.* If you are one, you will take no pleasure in those who aren't. Unhappy is the eminence that isn't founded on substance. There are more true men in appearance than in reality. There are fakers who conceive chimeras and give birth to deceits, and there are others, similar to them, who encourage them and prefer the uncertainty of deceit (which is much) to the certainty of truth (which is little). Their whims turn out badly, for they are not grounded on integrity. Only the truth can give you a true reputation, and only substance is profitable. One act of deceit calls for many others, and soon the whole ghastly construction, which is founded in the air, comes tumbling down. Unfounded things never reach old age. Their promises make them suspect, and their proofs make us reject them.

176 *Either know, or listen to someone who does.* To live, you need understanding: either your own, or borrowed. But many people are unaware that they do not know, and others think they know when

they do not. Attacks of foolishness have no remedy. Because the ignorant do not know themselves, they never look for what they're lacking. Some would be sages if they did not believe they were so already. Oracles of prudence are rare, but all of them are idle, for no one consults them. Asking advice won't diminish your greatness or cast doubt on your talent. To the contrary; it will strengthen your reputation. To combat misfortune, take counsel with reason.

177 *Don't grow too familiar with others*, or permit them to be so with you. You will lose the superiority your rectitude had given you, and with it your reputation. The stars do not brush against us, and thus they conserve their splendor. Divinity requires dignity, and familiarity breeds contempt. Human things, when most used, are least respected, for communication reveals the defects that reserve had hidden. Don't grow too familiar with anyone. Not with your superiors, for it is dangerous, nor with your inferiors, for it is undignified, and least of all with the rabble, which is foolish and insolent. Unable to realize you are doing them a favor, the rabble think it your obligation. Familiarity rhymes with vulgarity.

178 *Trust your heart*, especially when it is a strong one. Never contradict it, for usually it can predict the things that matter most: it is a homegrown oracle. Many perished from what they feared, but what good was fearing it when they took no steps to prevent it? Some people have a very loyal heart, given to them by nature, which always forewarns them and sounds the alarm, saving them from failure. It is not prudent to rush into troubles, but it is to meet them halfway, in order to conquer them.

179 *Reserve is the seal of talent.* A breast without reserve is an open letter. Have depths where you can hide your secrets: great spaces and little coves where important things can sink to the bottom and hide. Reserve comes from having mastered yourself, and being reserved is a genuine triumph. You pay tribute to as many people as you discover yourself to. The health of prudence lies in inner moderation. Reserve is threatened by others who feel you out, who contradict you to get a handle on you, or insinuate things that can make even the shrewdest give himself away. Neither say what you will do nor do what you have said.

180 *Never govern yourself by what your enemy ought to do.* The fool never does what the prudent person thinks he will, for he cannot understand that it is to his advantage. Nor will he do it if he is wise, for he will want to dissimulate his intent, which you may have discovered and planned for. Examine both sides of things; go back and forth between them. Try to remain impartial. Don't think about what *will* happen; think about what *could*.

181 *Don't lie, but don't tell the whole truth.* Nothing requires more skill than the truth, which is like a letting of blood from the heart. It takes skill both to speak it and to withhold it. A single lie can destroy your reputation for honesty. The man deceived seems faulty, and the deceiver seems false, which is worse. Not all truths can be spoken: some should be silenced for your own sake, others for the sake of someone else.

182 *Show everyone a bit of daring: an important sort of prudence.* Change your view of others:

don't think so highly of them that you fear them. Never let your imagination surrender to your heart. Many people seem great until you mingle with them, and communication leads more often to disappointment than to esteem. No one can exceed the narrow limits of humanity. Everyone's intellect and character has an "if only . . ." Rank bestows a certain apparent authority, but rarely is this accompanied by that of personal merit, for luck often punishes the person in a high position by giving him less talent. The imagination always rushes ahead and makes things out to be more than they are. It imagines not only what exists, but what might exist. Reason, drawing on experience, should see things clearly and correct her. Fools shouldn't be bold, nor the virtuous fearful. And if self-confidence helps the foolish and simple, how much more will it help the wise and courageous!

183 *Don't hold on to anything too firmly.* Fools are stubborn, and the stubborn are fools, and the more erroneous their judgment is, the more they hold on to it. Even when you are right, it is good to make concessions: people will recognize you were right but admire your courtesy. More is lost through holding on than can be won by defeating others. One defends not truth but rudeness. There are heads of

iron, difficult to convince, hopelessly obstinate. When whim meets stubbornness, they bond forever into foolishness. Be firm in will, not in judgment. There are exceptional cases, of course, when one shouldn't give in twice: once in judgment and once in execution.

184 *Don't stand on ceremony.* Even in kings, this affectation looks like eccentricity. The punctilious person is a nuisance, and there are entire countries stricken with this squeamishness. The clothes of fools—idolaters of their own honor—are held together with these silly stitches, and they show that their honor is based on little, for anything seems to offend it. It is good to demand respect but not to be taken for a paragon of affectation. It is true that a totally unceremonious person needs great talent to succeed. Courtesy should neither be exaggerated nor scorned. You don't show your greatness by paying attention to the fine points of honor.

185 *Don't risk your reputation on one roll of the dice.* If it comes out badly, the harm will be irreparable. You can easily err once, especially the first time. You aren't always at your best, and not every day is

yours. So let there be a second attempt to make up for the first . . . and if the first one goes right, it will redeem the second one. There must always be room for improvement and for appeal. Things depend on all sorts of circumstance, and luck grants us success only rarely.

186 *Know when something is a defect*, even if it looks like the opposite. Honesty should be able to recognize vice even when it dresses in brocade. Sometimes it wears a crown of gold, but even then it cannot hide its iron. Slavery is just as vile when disguised by high position. Vices can be elevated, but are always base. Some people see a certain hero with a certain fault, but they don't realize that it wasn't the fault that made him a hero. The example of people in high places is so persuasive that it makes others imitate even their ugliness. Adulation mimics even an ugly face, without realizing that what is hidden by greatness is abominated when greatness is lacking.

187 *When something pleases others, do it yourself. When it is odious, have someone else do it.* You will win favor, and shift ill will onto others. Great and noble people find it more pleasant to do good than to receive it. You can rarely trouble another without feeling troubled, either by pity or by remorse. In matters of reward or retribution let good be administered immediately, and bad, mediately, through another. You should give others something they can pummel with the hatred and gossip of their discontent. The anger of the rabble is like rabies. Without realizing what has harmed it, it snaps at the muzzle. And though the muzzle isn't to blame, it takes the immediate punishment.

188 *Find something to praise.* This will accredit your taste and tell others that you formed it on excellent things, making them hope for your esteem. If someone has found out what perfection is, he will value it wherever it appears. Praise offers subjects for conversation and for imitation. It is an urbane way to recommend courtesy to those who accompany you. Some people do the opposite: they always find something to criticize, flattering those present by scorning those absent. This works with superficial people who are unaware of the trick: speaking ill of one to speak ill of the other. Other people make it a habit to admire the mediocrities of today more than the eminences of yesterday. Let the prudent person see through both of these ruses, giving in neither to exaggeration nor to flattery. And let him realize that these critics take the same approach no matter whose company they are in.

189 *Utilize other people's privations.* When privation leads to desire, it gives us the surest way to manipulate others. Philosophers said that privation was nothing, and men of state say it is everything: the latter were right. Some people climb the steps of others' desires to reach their own ends. They take advantage of the tight spots others are in, and use difficulty to whet their appetite. They find the sting of want more useful than the complacency of possession, and as things grow more difficult, desire grows more vehement. A subtle way of getting what you want: maintain dependency.

190 *Find consolation in everything.* Even the useless have their consolation: they are eternal. There is no cloud without a silver lining. For fools it is being lucky. As the proverb says, "The beautiful wish they were as lucky as the ugly." To live much, it is good to be worth little. The glass that is cracked is the one that annoys us by never breaking completely. Fortune seems to envy the most important people. It rewards uselessness with endurance and importance with brevity. Those who matter will always be in short supply, and the person who is good for nothing will be eternal, either because he seems so, or really is. As for the unfortunate person, luck and death seem to conspire to forget him.

191 *Don't take payment in politeness.* It is a cheat. Some people, in order to cast a spell, have no need of magic potions. By doffing their hats the right way, they bewitch fools—the vain, that is. They sell honor, and pay their debts with a gust of fine words. He who promises everything promises nothing; promises are a trap for fools. True courtesy is a duty, false courtesy a deceit, and excessive courtesy isn't dignity but dependence. Those who practice it bow not to the person but to his wealth and to his flattery; not to good qualities, but to hoped-for favors.

192 *A peaceable person is a long-lived one.* To live, let live. Peaceable people not only live, they reign. Listen and see, but keep quiet. A day without

contention means a night of rest. To live much and to take pleasure in life is to live twice: the fruit of peace. You can have everything if you care little for what matters nothing. Nothing is sillier than to take everything seriously. It is just as foolish to let something wound you when it doesn't concern you as not to be wounded when it does.

193 *Beware of someone who pretends to put your interest before his own.* The best defence against guile is attentiveness. When people are subtle, be even more so. Some are good at making *their* business into yours, and if you don't decipher their intentions, you'll find yourself pulling their chestnuts out of the fire.

194 *Be realistic about yourself and your own affairs.* Even more so when you have just begun to live. Everyone thinks highly of himself, and those who are least think themselves the most. Everyone dreams of his fortune and imagines himself a prodigy. Hope seizes on something, and experience fails to deliver. A clear vision of reality is torture to a vain imagination. Be sensible. Want the best but expect the worst, so as to accept any outcome with equanimity. It is a good idea to aim a little high, but not so high as to miss the mark. When you begin a job, adjust your expectations. Where experience is lacking, presumptions often go wrong. Intelligence is a panacea for all sorts of foolishness. Know your radius of action and your condition and adjust your imagination to reality.

195

Know how to appreciate. There is no one who cannot better someone else at something, and there will always be someone who can conquer even him. It is useful to know exactly how to enjoy each person. The wise person esteems everyone, for he recognizes the good in each, and he realizes how hard it is to do things well. The fool despises others, partly out of ignorance and partly because he always prefers what is worst.

196

Know your lucky star. No one is so helpless as not to have one, and if you're unfortunate, it is because you haven't recognized it. Some people have access to princes and the powerful without really knowing how or why, and it is only that luck has favored them. It remains for them only to nurture their luck with effort. Others are favored by the wise. Certain people are better accepted in one country than in another, or better known in a certain city, and even among people of identical merit, some are luckier in certain pursuits. Luck shuffles the cards the way she wants to. Let each person know his own luck, and his own talents; losing and winning depend on it. Know how to follow your lucky star. Don't change it or give the boot to Boötes.*

197 *Never stumble over fools.* A fool is someone who doesn't recognize a fool, and, even more, someone who does, but doesn't get rid of him. Fools are dangerous to deal with, even superficially, and do much harm if you confide in them. For a while they are held back by their own caution or that of others, but the delay serves only to deepen their foolishness. Someone who has no reputation can do only harm to yours. Fools are always unfortunate—this is their burden—and their double misfortune sticks to them and rubs off on those they deal with. They have only one thing that isn't completely bad: although the wise

*That is, don't turn your back on that constellation if it contains your lucky star.

are of no use to them, they can be of use to the wise, as negative examples.

198 *Know how to transplant yourself.* There are entire peoples who are esteemed only after transplanting themselves, and this is especially true in high places. Mother countries behave like stepmothers toward the eminent. Envy finds fertile soil and reigns over everything, remembering one's initial imperfections rather than the greatness one reached later. A mere pin won esteem by traveling from the old world to the new, and a bead of glass made people scorn the diamond.* Everything foreign is held in esteem, whether it came from afar, or because people see it only after it is well formed and has reached perfection. Some people were scorned in their own little corner but achieved worldly eminence. They are honored by their own people because they look at them from a distance and by foreigners because they came from afar. The statue on the altar will never be venerated by someone who saw it back when it was a tree trunk in the forest.

*An allusion to the European exploration of the New World.

199 *Be prudent when you try to win esteem,* and don't do it by intruding. The true road to a good reputation is merit, and if effort builds upon worth, it can take a shortcut. Integrity alone is not enough, and neither is diligence, for your efforts can get you dirty enough to ruin your reputation. Steer a middle course: you should have merit but also know how to present yourself.

200 *Have something to hope for,* so as not to be happily unhappy. The body breathes and the spirit yearns for things. If all were possession, all would be disappointment and discontent. Even the understanding needs something else to learn, something curiosity can feed on. Hope gives us life, but gorging on happiness can be fatal. When rewarding others, never leave them satisfied. When they want nothing, you should fear everything: unhappy happiness. Fear begins where desire ends.

201 *Fools are all those who look like fools, and half of those who do not.* Idiocy has taken over the

world; if anything remains of wisdom, it is foolishness in the eyes of the divinity. The greatest fool is the one who doesn't think *himself* one, only others. To be wise, it isn't enough to look wise and, even less, seem wise to yourself. You know when you think you don't know, and you don't see when you don't see that others do. The world is filled with fools, but none of them considers himself one, or tries not to be one.

202 *Words and deeds make a perfect man.* Speak what is very good, do what is very honorable. The first shows a perfect head, the second a perfect heart, and both arise in a superior spirit. Words are the shadows of deeds. Words are female, and deeds are male. Better to be celebrated than to celebrate others; it is easy to speak and difficult to act. Deeds are the substance of life, and wise sayings the adornment. Eminence endures in deeds but perishes in words. Actions are the fruit of prudent reflection. Words are wise, deeds are mighty.

203 *Know the great men of your age.* They are not many. One Phoenix in all the world, one Great Captain, one perfect orator, one wise man per century, one eminent king in many. Mediocrities abound and win little esteem. Eminences are rare, for they require total perfection, and the higher the category, the harder it is to reach it. Many have called themselves "great," borrowing the name from Caesar and Alexander, but in vain; without deeds, that word is only a puff of air. There have been few Senecas, and only one Apelles won enduring fame.

204 *Undertake the easy as though it were difficult, and the difficult as though it were easy*, so as not to grow overconfident or discouraged. To avoid doing something, you need only consider it done. But diligence conquers impossibility. In moments of great danger, don't even think, simply act. Don't dwell on the difficulties.

205 *Learn to use scorn.* One way to get things is to scorn them. When you look for them, they aren't there, and later, without your trying, they come running. Earthly things are the shadows of heavenly ones, and they behave like shadows; they flee when you pursue them and chase you when you flee them. Scorn is also the shrewdest way to take revenge. A wise maxim: Never defend yourself with the pen, for this leaves a trail and glorifies your rivals rather than punishing them for their insolence. Unworthy people cunningly oppose the great: they try to win fame indirectly, without really deserving it. Many people would be unknown if their excellent opponents had paid them no heed. There is no revenge like oblivion: burying others in the dust of their inanity. Impudent fools, they try to become immortal by setting fire to the wonders of the world and of the centuries. One way to quiet vulgar murmuring is to ignore it. To impugn it will harm you. To give it credit brings discredit on you. Be happy that people want to emulate you, though their breath can tarnish, if not blacken, the greatest perfection.

206 *Know that there are vulgar people everywhere*, even in Corinth,* and even in the most distinguished family. Everyone experiences it in his own home. Not only are there vulgar people, there are high-born vulgarians, who are even worse. These people reflect the qualities of the vulgar, as in the pieces of a broken mirror, but do more harm. They speak

---

*Corinth is mentioned as a symbol of learning and refinement.

like fools and impudently criticize others. Great disciples of ignorance, godfathers of idiocy, avid for degrading gossip. Pay no attention to what they say, and less to what they feel. Know them, yes, in order to avoid them: avoid taking part in their vulgarity or being its object. Any foolishness is vulgarity, and the vulgar are composed of fools.

207   *Use self-control.* Be especially alert towards chance events. The sudden movements of the passions throw prudence off balance, and here is where you can be lost. You move more in a single moment of furor or content than you do in many hours of indifference. Run amuck for only a second and you will run up lifelong regrets. Cunning people set these traps for prudence in order to sound matters out and fathom the minds of their opponents. Prying out secrets, they get to the bottom of the greatest talents. Your counter-strategy? Control yourself, especially your sudden impulses. It takes much reflection to keep a passion from bolting like a horse; and if you're wise on horseback, you're wise in everything. The person who foresees danger feels his way along. A word uttered in passion may be light to the person who hurled it but should feel heavy to the one who catches and ponders it.

208 *Don't die from an attack of foolishness.* Wise men commonly die insane. Fools choke to death on advice. You die of foolishness when you reason too much. Some die because they feel everything, others because they feel nothing. Some are fools because they suffer no regrets, and others because they do. It is foolish to perish from excessive intelligence. Some perish because they understand everything, and others live because they understand nothing. Although many die of foolishness, few fools ever really die, for few ever begin to live.

209 *Free yourself from common foolishness.* This requires a special sort of sanity. Common foolishness is authorized by custom, and some people who resisted the ignorance of individuals were unable to resist that of the multitude. The vulgar are never happy with their luck, even when it is best, or unhappy with intellect, even when it is the worst. Unhappy with their own happiness, they covet that of others. People of today praise things of yesterday, and those who are here, the things that are there. The past seems better, and everything distant is held more dear. The person who laughs at everything is just as foolish as the one made wretched by everything.

210 *Know how to handle truth.* The truth is dangerous, but a good person cannot fail to speak it. This requires artifice. The skilled physicians of the mind invented truth-sweeteners, for when truth is used to give someone the lie, it is quintessentially bitter. This takes consummate skill and the right manner. With the very same truth, one person flatters, and another batters, our ears. Speak to those present in the past. When you're dealing with someone intelligent, it is enough to allude to things, or use no words at all. Princes should never be given bitter cures. To disillusion them, gild the pill.

211 *In heaven all is contentment, in hell all is sorrow, and on earth, which is in between, we find both.* We live between two extremes and partake of both. Luck changes: not all is happiness and not all is adversity. This life is a zero: by itself it is nothing. Add the heavens, and it is much. Indifference to the world's variety is prudence; the wise care little for novelty. Our lives fold and unfold like theater, so be careful to end well.

212 *Never reveal the final stratagems of your art.* Great teachers are subtle about the way they reveal their subtleties. Preserve your superiority and remain a teacher. Use art when you reveal your art. Don't dry up the sources of your teaching or your giving. That way you will preserve your reputation and keep others dependent on you. Both in teaching and in granting others what they want, you should bait people's admiration and reveal perfection little by little. Reserve has always been a great rule for living and for winning, especially in matters of importance.

213 *Know how to contradict.* It is a great way to provoke others: they commit themselves and you commit nothing. You can use contradiction to pry loose the passions of others. Showing disbelief makes people vomit up their secrets; it is the key to tightly closed breasts. With great subtlety you can test the will and judgment of others. Shrewdly scorn the word that someone else has cloaked in mystery, and you will hunt down his deepest secrets and make them come little by little to his tongue, where they can be trapped in the nets of subtle deceit. The prudent person's reserve makes others lose theirs. It discovers their feelings when their hearts should have been in-

scrutable. A feigned doubt is the best skeleton key your curiosity can have: it will find out all it wants. Even when it comes to learning, the good student contradicts his teacher and makes him more eager to explain and defend the truth. Challenge someone discreetly and his teaching will be more perfect.

214

Don't turn one act of foolishness into two. Often we commit four to correct one. They say that one lie leads to another, greater one, and it is the same with folly. It is always bad to back the wrong cause, and worse still not to know how to hide your error. Imperfection is taxing, but you will pay still more dearly if you defend and increase it. The greatest of sages can commit one mistake, but not two: he may fall into error, but he doesn't lie down and make his home there.

215

Pay attention to the person with hidden intentions. The shrewd person distracts someone's will in order to attack it. Once it wavers it is easily defeated. These people conceal their intentions in order to get what they want and put themselves second in order to come out first. Their aim is best when no one sees them take aim. Stay awake as long as intentions do. When intentions go into hiding, redouble your vigilance. Be careful to penetrate the scheming of others. Watch them dart to and fro in order to home in on what they want. They propose one thing and intend another, flying in circles before their intentions come home to roost. Be cautious of their concessions. Sometimes it is best to make others understand that you have understood.

216   *Express yourself clearly*: not only easily but lucidly. Some people conceive well but give birth badly, for without clarity, the children of the soul—concepts, resolutions—never see the light. Some people resemble drinking vessels that absorb much but give off little, while others say even more than they feel. What resolution is to the will, clarity is to the intellect: both are great gifts. People of lucid understanding are acclaimed, the confused have often been venerated for being incomprehensible, and, in fact, sometimes it is good to be obscure, so as not to be vulgar. But how will others understand what they are hearing if we ourselves have no clear idea what we are saying?

217 *Neither love nor hate forever.* Treat your friends as though they could become your worst enemies. Since this happens in reality, let it happen in foresight. We shouldn't give arms to the turncoats of friendship; they will wage the worst sort of war with them. On the contrary, when it comes to enemies, leave the door open to reconciliation. The door of gallantry is the surest one. The pleasure of revenge often turns into torment, and the satisfaction of having harmed someone often turns to pain.

218 *Never do something out of stubbornness, only out of attentive reflection.* Any obstinacy is evil—the daughter of passion, who never got anything right. There are some who turn everything into warfare, who behave like social bandits and would like to conquer others in all they do. They have no idea how to live peaceably. These people are particularly harmful as rulers. They divide the government into factions and make enemies out of those who should be as obedient as children. They want to do everything through stealth, and attribute their success to their own scheming. But once others discover their paradoxical humor, they grow angry with them and block them in their chimerical pursuits, and thus they achieve nothing. They cannot digest all their troubles and others take pleasure in their bellyaches. Their judgment is damaged, and sometimes their hearts. The way to deal with such monsters is to flee civilization and dwell among savages. For the barbarism of savages is more bearable than the savagery of these barbarians.

219 *Don't be known for your artifice*, though you can no longer live without it. Better prudent than astute. Everyone likes to be treated squarely, but not everyone likes to treat others that way. Don't let sincerity turn into simplicity, or shrewdness into cunning. Better to be venerated as wise than feared as stealthy. Sincere people are loved, but often deceived. The best artifice is to conceal it, for artifice is taken as deceit. Plainness flourished in the age of gold, and malice in this age of iron. It is an honor to be considered a capable person; it inspires confidence. But to be thought astute rouses suspicions of sophistry.

220 *If you can't wear the skin of a lion, wear the skin of a fox.* To follow the times is to lead them.

If you get what you want, your reputation will not suffer. If you lack strength, use skill; take one road or the other, the royal road of courage or the shortcut of artifice. Know-how has accomplished more than strength, and the wise have conquered the courageous more often than vice versa. When you can't get what you want, you risk being despised.

221 *Don't be hotheaded*, putting yourself or others at risk. Some people are obstacles to their own dignity, and to that of others. They are always on the verge of foolishness. They are easy to find and difficult to get along with. They are not content with a hundred annoyances a day. Everything rubs them the wrong way, and they contradict as many people as they rub up against. They put their judgment on backward and disapprove of everything. But those who most try our prudence are those who do nothing well and speak ill of everything. The land of discontent is a spacious one, filled with monsters.

222 *Cautious hesitation is a sign of prudence.* The tongue is a wild animal, and once it breaks loose, it is hard to return it to its cage. It is the pulse of the

soul. The wise use it to test our health; the attentive, to listen to the heart. The trouble is that the person who ought to be the most cautious is often the least. The wise avoid troublesome, compromising situations, and show their self-mastery. The wise person is circumspect: a Janus of equity, an Argos of watchfulness. A better Momus* would have wanted eyes on the hands rather than a window in the breast.

223 *Don't be eccentric.* Either out of affectation or because they don't notice, many people have notable eccentricities, and do whimsical things that are more defects than signs of distinction. Some people are known for a singularly ugly facial blemish, but eccentric people are known for a certain excess in the way they handle themselves. Being eccentric will only ruin your reputation. Your own special impertinence will rouse laughter in some and annoyance in others.

224 *Know how to take things.* Never against the grain, though they're handed to you that way. There are two sides to everything. If you grab the

*Momus censured Hephaestus for having formed a man without leaving a little door in the breast that would enable others to look into his secret thoughts.

blade, the best thing will do you harm; the most harmful will defend you if you seize it by the hilt. Many things that caused pain could have caused pleasure if only their advantages had been considered. There are always pros and cons; the trick lies in knowing how to turn things to your advantage. Things look different when seen in a different light. So look at them in the light of happiness. Don't confuse good and bad. This is why some people find contentment in everything, and others sorrow. This is a sure defense against the reversals of fortune, and a great rule for living, at all times and in every pursuit.

225 *Know your major defect.* Every talent is balanced by a fault, and if you give in to it, it will govern you like a tyrant. You can begin to overthrow it by paying heed to it: begin to conquer it by identifying it. Pay it the same attention as those who reproach you for it. To master yourself, you must reflect upon yourself. Once this imperfection has surrendered, all others will follow.

226 *Be sure to win people's favor.* Many people behave not according to who they are but the way they're obliged to. Anyone can convince us of the

bad, for the bad is easily believed, though sometimes it seems incredible. The best and most we have depends on the respect of others. Some are content to be right, but it is not enough: one must also be diligent. Pleasing others costs little and is worth much. Deeds are bought with words. There is no trifling utensil in the house of the universe that isn't needed at least once a year. It is worth little, but much needed. Remember that when people speak about things, they follow their feelings.

227 *Don't surrender to first impressions.* Some people marry the first information they receive, and turn what comes later into their concubine. Since deceit is always first to arrive, there is no room left for truth. Don't fill up your will with the first goal that occurs to you, nor your intelligence with the first proposition: it will show you have no depth. Some people are like new drinking vessels: they soak up the first aroma to reach them, whether the liquor is good or bad. When others learn of this limitation, they begin to scheme maliciously. Those with bad intentions dye credulity whatever color they want. There should always be time to look something over twice. Alexander kept his other ear for the other side of the story. Pay attention to your second and third

informants. To be easily impressed shows a lack of
depth and it is close to passion.

228 *Don't be a scandal sheet.* Don't be
known for impugning the fame of others. Don't be
witty at someone else's expense: it is more odious
than difficult. All will take revenge and speak ill of
you, and since you are one and others are many, you'll
be easily defeated. Take no content in the ills of
others, and don't comment on them. A gossip is
always detested. He may mingle with great people,
but they will value him as a source of amusement,
not of prudence. And he who speaks ill hears worse.

229 *Parcel out your life wisely.* Not confusedly, in the rush of events, but with foresight and judgment. Life is painful without a rest, like a long day's
journey without an inn. What makes life pleasant is
a variety of learning. For a beautiful life, spend the
first act in conversation with the dead: we are born
to know and to know ourselves, and books turn us
faithfully into people. Spend the second act with the
living: behold all that is good in the world. Not all
things are found in one region. In distributing the

dowry, the universal Father sometimes gave wealth to his ugliest daughter. The third act belongs entirely to you: to philosophize is the highest delight of all.

230 *Open your eyes before it is too late*. Not all who see have opened their eyes, nor all who look, see. To realize something too late brings no relief, only sorrow. Some start to see when there is nothing left to see: they lost their homes and affairs before they found themselves. It is hard to give understanding to someone with no will, and more difficult to give will to someone with no understanding. People circle these people like blind men, mocking them. Because they are deaf to advice, they do not open their eyes to see. Some people encourage this blindness: they *are* because others are not. It is an unlucky horse whose owner has no eyes. He will never grow sleek.

231 *Never show half-finished things to others*. Let them be enjoyed in their perfection. All beginnings are formless, and what lingers is the image of that deformity. The memory of having seen something imperfect spoils our enjoyment when it is fin-

ished. To take in a large object at a single glance keeps us from appreciating the parts, but it satisfies our taste. Before it *is*, everything it is not, and when it begins to be, it is still very close to nonbeing. It is revolting to watch even the most succulent dish being cooked. Great teachers are careful not to let their works be seen in embryo. Learn from nature, and don't show them until they look good.

232 *Have a touch of the practical.* Not everything should be speculation; you must also act. The wisest are easiest to deceive: they may know extraordinary things, but they know nothing of life's ordinary necessities. The contemplation of sublime things keeps them from lowly, easy ones, and because they don't know the first things about living—an area where everyone else is so sharp—they are either marveled over or considered ignorant by the superficial crowd. So let the wise have a touch of the practical, enough not to be deceived and mocked. Know how to get things done: it may not be the highest thing in life, but it is the most necessary. What good is knowledge if it isn't practical? These days true knowledge lies in knowing how to live.

233 *Don't mistake other people's tastes*, giving pain instead of pleasure. Some people try to win favor and end up being annoying, for they don't understand the character of others. The same thing flatters some and insults others. What you thought a service turns into an offense. Sometimes it would have taken less trouble to please than it did to annoy. You lose the gratitude and ruin the gift when you've lost all direction in pleasing others. If you don't understand someone else's character, you won't be able to satisfy him. This is why some people think they are praising and are really being insulting: a well-deserved punishment. Others think they are flattering us with their eloquence, and they are really battering our souls with their gab.

234 *If you trust your honor to someone else, keep his in pledge.* The penalty for speaking too much and the advantages of silence should be the same for both of you. Where honor is involved, all must share the same interests, and one's own reputation should make one look out for that of others. It's better not to confide in others, but if you do, arrange matters skillfully so that your confidant will show not only

prudence but caution. Share the risk, so that both of you are obeying a common interest and your confidant will not turn into a witness against you.

235 *Know how to ask.* There is nothing more difficult for some, or easier for others. There are some who do not know how to say no; you need no lever, no skeleton key to deal with them. Others say no automatically, and here you need effort. With all of them, do things at the right moment. Catch them when they are in good spirits, after their minds or bodies have been feasting, unless, of course, they are attentive enough to penetrate your intent. Days of pleasure are those when people do favors; for joy flows from the inner man to the outer. Don't draw near when you see somebody else being refused something, for there is no longer any fear of saying no. Nor will you gain anything from the sad. Placing people in your debt beforehand is good currency, unless they are base and vile and feel no obligation to return a favor.

236 *Turn someone's reward into a favor.* It is a shrewd policy. Bestowing favors rather than simply rewarding merit shows a certain nobility. Favors done quickly are twice as excellent. Something given early is more binding to the receiver. And second, obligation turns into gratitude. This is a subtle transformation: you begin by paying a debt and end up passing it on to your creditor. This works only among well-bred people. Among knaves, the honorarium paid beforehand acts as a bit, not as a spur.

237 *Never share your secrets with those greater than you.* You may think you'll share pears, but you'll share only the parings. Many perished by being confidants. They were like the spoons made from bread crusts, and came to the same quick end. To hear a prince's secrets isn't a privilege but a burden. Many smash the mirror that reminds them of their ugliness. They can't stand to see those who saw them. You won't be seen well if you've seen something unfavorable. You should never hold anyone greatly in your debt, especially not the powerful. And hold them with favors you've done, not with those you've received. The confidences of friends are the most dangerous of all. The person who tells his secrets to another makes himself a slave, and this is a violence that the sovereign cannot bear. To recover their lost freedom they will trample on everything, even reason. Secrets? Neither hear them nor speak them.

238 *Know what piece you are missing.* Many would be complete people if they had the piece they needed to reach the height of perfect being. Some would be much if they paid attention to very little. Some lack seriousness, and this darkens great talents. Others lack gentleness, which is something their friends and family miss very quickly, especially when they hold power. Some lack quick execution, and others the ability to stop and meditate. If they noticed these defects, they could easily make up for them. For care can turn habit into a second nature.

239 *Don't be overly clever.* Better to be prudent. If you sharpen your wits too much, you will miss the point, or break your point: that is what happens to common subtlety. Common sense is safer. It is good to be intelligent, but not to be a pedant. Much reasoning is a kind of disputing. Better a substantial judgment that reasons only as much as it needs to.

240 *Make use of folly.* Even the wisest person sometimes puts this piece into play, and there are

occasions when the greatest knowledge lies in appearing to have none. You needn't be ignorant, only pretend to be so. Wisdom matters little to fools, and madmen care little for sanity. So speak to everyone in his own tongue. The fool isn't the person who pretends to be foolish, but the one who is, for there is no foolishness where there is artifice. To be admired by others, wear the hide of an ass.

241 *Allow yourself to be joked about, but don't joke about others.* The first is a sort of courtesy, but the second will get you into difficulties. The person who is ill-humored at a party is even more of a beast than he appears to be. Excellent jokes are pleasant, and to know how to take them is a sign of talent. If you show you are piqued, you'll make others pick at you again. There is a moment to stop joking and not provide occasion for more. The most serious problems have arisen from joking. There is nothing that requires more attention and skill. Before you begin, know how much someone else can take.

242 *Follow through on your victories.* Some people do everything to begin and nothing to end.

Fickle characters, they start but don't persist. They never win praise because they carry on but don't carry through. To them everything is over before it ends. The Spaniard is known for his impatience, as the Belgian is for his patience. The latter finishes things, the former finishes them off; he sweats until he has conquered difficulty, is content to conquer, but doesn't know how to carry through on his victory. He proves that he *can* but doesn't *want* to. This is always a defect: it shows either inconstancy or having rashly attempted the impossible. What is worth doing is worth finishing. If it isn't worth finishing, why begin at all? The wise don't merely stalk their prey, they make the kill.

243 *Don't be all dove.* Let the guile of the serpent alternate with the innocence of the dove. No one is easier to fool than a good man; the person who never lies believes others easily, and the one who never deceives trusts others. Being fooled isn't always a sign of foolishness; sometimes it shows goodness. Two kinds of people are good at foreseeing danger: those who have learned at their own expense and the clever people who learn a great deal at the expense of others. You should be as cautious at foreseeing difficulties as you are shrewd at getting out of them. Don't be so

good that you give others the chance to be bad. Be part serpent and part dove; not a monster, but a prodigy.

244 *Place others in your debt*. Some people disguise their own profit as the profit of others: they make it appear they are granting a favor when they are really receiving one. Some are so shrewd that they bestow honor by asking a favor; and they honor others with their own gain. They arrange things so that others seem to be paying them their due when they give them something. Extraordinarily clever, they scramble the order of doing favors and cast doubt upon who is favoring whom. They buy the best things with simple praise. By showing they like something, they bestow honor and flattery. They stake a claim on the courtesy of others, making a debt out of something they themselves should have felt grateful for. They use the verb *oblige* in the active voice rather than in the passive, and are better at politics than at grammar. This is a great subtlety, but it is even more subtle to catch someone doing it, undo the exchange, return someone's honor, and recover the advantage.

245 *Sometimes you should reason with uncommon sense.* It betokens a superior talent. Don't think highly of the person who never opposes you. It doesn't show that he loves you, it shows he loves himself. Don't be fooled by flattery: don't reward it, condemn it. Consider it an honor to be criticized, especially by those who speak ill of good people. You should be pained when your things please everyone; it is a sign that they are not good, for perfection belongs to only a few.

246 *Don't give explanations to those who haven't asked for them.* And although they *are* asked for, it is folly to give them too eagerly. To offer excuses before they are called for is to incriminate yourself, and to bleed yourself when you are healthy is to attract malady and malice. Excusing yourself beforehand awakens suspicions that were fast asleep. The prudent person should never blink before the suspicions of others: that would be looking for offense. He should try to dissimulate with a firm, righteous manner.

247 *Know a little more, live a little less*. Some say the opposite. The right kind of leisure is better than the wrong kind of work. We have nothing to call our own but time, the only abode of the helpless and homeless. Life is precious, and it is as foolish to spend it on mechanical tasks as to spend too much of it on lofty ones. Burden yourself neither with occupations nor with envy. You will trample on life and suffocate the spirit. Some extend this principle to knowledge, but one cannot live if one doesn't know.

248 *Don't be obsessed with the latest*. Impertinence always goes to extremes, and there are people who only believe the latest thing they've heard.* Their senses and desires are made of wax: whatever it is, the "latest" impresses them and wipes out all that went before. These people are as easily won as lost. Everyone paints them a different color. They are bad confidants: children who never grow up. Fickle in their judgments and affections, they are always in flux, with a limping will and judgment, tilting this way or that.

*The other extreme is to believe the first thing you hear. See aphorism 227.

249 *Don't start living when you should be ending.* Some rest at the beginning and leave their efforts and fatigue for last. Do the essential things first, and later, if there is time, those that are accessory. Some want to triumph before they struggle. Others begin their studies with what matters least, and postpone what can bring renown and usefulness until the end of their lives. Some people grow vain as soon as they have begun to make their fortune. Method is essential in knowing and in living.

250 *When should we reason backward?* When we are spoken to with malice. Some people reverse everything: yes is no and no is yes. If they criticize something, it means they think highly of it. Because they covet it for themselves, they try to discredit it for others. Not all praise involves speaking well. Some people avoid praising the good by praising the bad. If someone finds no one bad, he can find no one good.

251 *Use human means as though divine ones didn't exist, and divine means as though there were no*

human ones. A great master* gave that advice, and it requires no comment.

252 *Live neither entirely for yourself nor entirely for others*. It is a vulgar sort of tyranny. If you want to belong entirely to yourself, you'll want everything for yourself. Such people don't know how to yield, even in the smallest things, or give up even a tiny bit of their own comfort. They never win other people's favor; they trust in their fortune, and acquire a false sense of security. It is good to belong to others at times so that others can belong to you. If you hold public office, you must be a public slave. Either bear the burden or give up the berth, as the old woman said to Hadrian. Some people belong entirely to others, for foolishness always deals in excess, and this is a very unhappy sort of excess. They have not a day, not an hour to call their own, so completely do they give themselves to others. This is true even in matters of understanding. Some people know everything for others and nothing for themselves. If you are prudent, you will understand that people seek you not for your own sake but for their own. What interests them is what you can do for them.

*Saint Ignatius of Loyola (1491–1556), founder of the Society of Jesus.

253 *Don't express your ideas too clearly.* Most people think little of what they understand, and venerate what they do not. To be valued, things must be difficult: if they can't understand you, people will think more highly of you. To win respect, make yourself seem wiser and more prudent than is required by the person you are dealing with. But do so with moderation. Intelligent people value brains, but most people demand a certain elevation. Keep them guessing at your meaning, and don't give them a chance to criticize you. Many praise without being able to say why. They venerate anything hidden or mysterious, and they praise it because they hear it praised.

254 *Don't scorn an evil because it is a small one*, for they never come alone, but always in a chain, as does happiness. Fortune and misfortune are usually drawn to where they already abound. Most people flee from the unfortunate and draw near the fortunate. Even doves, for all their simplicity, fly to the whitest dovecote. The unfortunate person has nothing: he is lacking himself, his reason, and any sort of consolation. Don't awaken unhappiness when it is asleep. A slip means little at first, but then comes the fatal, endless fall. For just as no good was ever completely fulfilled, no bad was ever completely over. Face heaven-sent misfortune with patience and the earthly sort with prudence.

255 *Know how to do good.* A little bit at a time, but often. Don't bestow more favor on someone than he can return. He who gives much doesn't give; he sells. Don't exhaust the gratitude of others. When grateful people are unable to respond, they break off the correspondence. To lose them, you have only to place them too greatly in your debt. When they don't want to pay, they draw away, and turn into enemies. The idol doesn't want to see the sculptor who carved him, and the person who receives a favor would rather lose sight of the person who did it. So learn this subtle lesson about giving: if the gift is to be appreciated, it should be much desired but cost little.

256 *Be prepared.* For the rude, the stubborn, the vain, and for all sorts of fools. There are many of them, and prudence lies in avoiding them altogether. Make a few resolutions each day before the mirror of your prudence, and you will fend off their attacks. Use some foresight, and don't risk your reputation to vulgar happenstance. The person armed with prudence will not be attacked by folly. Human relations are full of sharp reefs where your reputation can run aground. The safest way is to change course, asking Ulysses for cleverness. This is where artful evasion comes in. And above all, use generosity and courtesy, the shortest way out of difficulty.

257 *Stop short of breaking off*, or your reputation will be shattered. Anyone makes a good enemy, but not everyone can be a good friend. Few can do good, and almost everyone bad. The day he broke with the beetle, even the eagle didn't feel safe nestling in the bosom of Jupiter.* Say things too abruptly and you will stir up the wrath of hypocrites, who were waiting for their chance. Friends whom you have offended make the bitterest enemies: to their own pet fault they add all of yours. When others observe us splitting up with someone, they speak as they feel and feel as they desire. They criticize our behavior either at the beginning of the friendship (for lack of providence) or at the end (for having waited so long). If you can't help but part company, do it gently and

*Allusion to Aesop's fable of the eagle and the beetle.

excusably, with a slackening of favor rather than a violent outburst. This is where the maxim about a fine withdrawal* comes in handy.

258 *Look for someone to help bear your misfortunes.* You will never be alone, not even in risky situations, and you won't have to bear all the hatred of others. Some people want to take charge of everything and all they do is take all the criticism. So have someone that can pardon you or help you bear hardship. Neither fortune nor the rabble are as quick to attack two people. Physicians, having mistaken the cure, are not mistaken to consult someone else who can help them carry the coffin. They share the weight and the sorrow, for misfortune borne alone is doubly intolerable.

259 *Foresee affronts and turn them into favors.* It is wiser to avoid them than to avenge them. It is a great skill to turn a potential rival into a confidant. Those who would have attacked your reputation become its protectors. It is valuable to know

*Aphorism 38.

how to place others in your debt and transform insult into gratitude. To turn sorrows into pleasures is to know how to live. Make malevolence itself your confidant.

260 *You can't belong entirely to others, and no one can be entirely yours.* Blood relations are not enough, nor friendship, nor even the most pressing sense of obligation; for it is very different to give someone your heart and to give him your will. Even the closest union has its exceptions. No matter how close you are to someone, the laws of politeness are in order. We keep one secret or another from our friend, and even a son does not reveal everything to his father. You withhold from some the things you communicate to others, and vice versa, so that you confess everything and withhold everything, depending on your confidant.

261 *Don't persist in folly.* Some people commit themselves to their errors. They act mistakenly and consider it constancy to go on that way. Deep inside, they accuse themselves; but they excuse themselves to everyone else. When they began to act fool-

ishly, people thought them careless; when they continue to do so, they are confirmed as fools. Neither the promise carelessly given nor the mistaken resolution should bind us forever. Some people prolong their stupidity and press forward with their short-sightedness. They want to be faithful fools.

262 *Know how to forget.* It takes more luck than skill. The things that should most be forgotten are the ones most easily remembered. Not only does memory behave basely, not coming forward when it is needed, it is also foolish, for it comes to us when it shouldn't. It is prolix when it can give us pain, and careless when it can give us pleasure. Sometimes the best remedy for troubles is to forget them, but we forget the remedy. Let us train the memory and teach it better manners, for it can give us heaven or hell. Self-satisfied people never care about this—in their silly innocence they are always happy.

263 *Many pleasant things are better when they belong to someone else.* You can enjoy them more that way. The first day, pleasure belongs to the owner; after that, to others. When things belong to others,

we enjoy them twice as much: without the risk of losing them, and with the pleasure of novelty. Everything tastes better when we are deprived of it; even someone else's water seems like nectar. Having your own things diminishes enjoyment, and increases your annoyance: at having to lend them, or not lend them. When you have things, you are really maintaining them for others, and more enemies will benefit from them than friends.

264 *Don't have days when you are careless.* Sometimes Luck likes to play a practical joke, and it will seize any opportunity to catch you off guard. Intelligence, prudence, courage, and even wisdom have to be ready for the test. The day they feel most confident will be the day they are most discredited. Caution is always most lacking when it is most needed. "I never thought of it" is what trips us up and casts us down. Those who observe us carefully use this stratagem, catching our perfections off guard as they scrutinize and take stock of us. They know the days on which we display our gifts; on those days cunning pays no heed. They choose the day we least expect to put us to the test.

265 *Get those who depend on you into tough situations.* A risky situation, at the right moment, has made many people into true persons: it is when you are drowning that you learn to swim. In this way many discovered what they were worth and how much they knew, and all this would otherwise have remained buried in timidity. Difficult situations give us the chance to win renown, and when a noble person finds his honor at risk, he can do more than a thousand others. This lesson (like so many others) was known very well by Isabel, the Catholic monarch, and to this timely favor, the Great Captain owes his renown, and many others their eternal fame. In this subtle way, she made great men.

266 *Don't be bad by being too good.* You will be, if you never get angry. Those who feel nothing are not really people. They don't always act that way out of insensitivity but often out of stupidity. To feel strongly, when circumstances call for it, makes you a person. Even birds poke fun at scarecrows. To alternate the bitter with the sweet shows good taste: sweetness alone is for children and fools. It is a great evil to be so insensible that you lose yourself by being good.

267 *Silken words, delivered gently.* Arrows go through the body: bad words, through the soul. A good lozenge makes the mouth smell good. To sell air is a subtle skill. Most things are paid for in words, and they alone can get you out of an impossible situation. When people are puffed up or have their heads in the clouds, you can use air to deal with them. The breath of a sovereign is especially persuasive. Have your mouth full of sugar, and make words into candy even your enemies will like. The only way to be loved is to be gentle and pleasant.

268 *The wise do sooner what fools do later.* Both do the same; all that differs is the *when*. The former act at the right moment, the latter at the wrong. If you start out by putting your intelligence on backward, you'll do everything else that way: trample under foot what you should have kept in your head, turn right into left, and act left-handedly. There is only one good way to see the light: as soon as possible. Otherwise, you do out of necessity what you might have done with pleasure. The wise size up immediately what has to be done, sooner or later, and do it with pleasure, enhancing their reputation.

269 *Take advantage of your novelty.* You will be esteemed as long as you are new. Novelty pleases everyone because of its variety. Our taste feels refreshed. A brand-new mediocrity is more highly regarded than an extremely talented person to whom we have grown accustomed. When eminences mingle with us they age more quickly. And remember that the glory of novelty lasts little. In four days people will lose their respect for you. Take advantage of the first fruits of esteem, and as they flee, snatch whatever you can. Once the warmth of novelty has died away, passion grows cold, and pleasure turns to irritation. Never doubt that all things had their season, and passed away.

270 *Don't be the only one to condemn what is popular.* There has to be something good about it, for it pleases so many, and—however inexplicably—is enjoyed. Eccentricity is always odious: when wrong, ridiculous. Scorn something that is popular and you'll be scorned yourself, and left alone with your bad taste. If you don't know how to find what's good, hide your dullness, and don't condemn things en masse; for bad taste is usually born from ignorance. What everyone says either *is* or wants to be.

271 *If you know little, stick to what is surest in each profession*. They may not consider you ingenious, but they'll think you solid. The person who knows can take risks and indulge his fantasy, but if you take risks knowing nothing, you will fall voluntarily. Keep to the right; what is tried and tested cannot fail. For those who know little, the main highway. Whether you know or don't, sureness is safer than eccentricity.

272 *Add courtesy to the price of what you're selling*: you will make others feel more obliged. The selfish person's request is no match for the gift of the generous and grateful. Courtesy doesn't simply give, it binds others. And gallantry makes us feel more obliged still. For a noble person, there is nothing more expensive than what is given to him free. You sell it twice and at two different prices: its own worth and that of courtesy. To the villainous, gallantry is gibberish, for they do not understand the language of good breeding.

273 *Understand the characters of the people you are dealing with* in order to penetrate their intentions. When you know the cause, you know the effect. The effect tells us the motive. The melancholy person always forecasts unhappiness, and the gainsayer, faults. They think only of the worst, and, overlooking the good that is present, they announce the evil that is possible. The person swayed by passion cannot speak of things as they are: passion speaks in him, not reason. Each person speaks according to his emotion or his humor, and all are far from the truth. You should know how to decipher a face and spell out the lettering of somebody's soul. Know that the person who is always laughing is a fool, and the one who never laughs is false. Be careful of the person who is always questioning you, either because he asks too much or because he carps and scruples. Expect little good from the person with a nasty face. These people like to avenge themselves on nature, because she honored them so little. A person is usually as foolish as he is beautiful.

274 *Be charming.* It is a wise sort of bewitchment. Let charm and courtesy capture the goodwill of others, and also their services. It isn't enough to have merit if you don't please others—this is what makes people praise you, and acclaim is the most useful instrument we have for ruling others. You are fortunate if others find you charming, but this must be helped by artifice, which works best when natural gifts are present. Charm leads to benevolence and, eventually, universal favor.

275 *Row with the current, but preserve your dignity.* Don't always look grave or annoyed. It is a sort of courtesy. You must yield a bit of your decorum to win popular favor. At times you can take the path of the many, but do so without losing dignity: the person taken for a fool in public will not be taken for a wise man in private. More is lost on a day of joking than was won with years of total gravity. Don't always be the odd man out. To be eccentric is to condemn others. And don't be squeamish and oversensitive; that is for women. Even squeamishness in spiritual matters is ridiculous. The best part of being a man is to seem like one. Women can imitate masculine qualities, but men shouldn't imitate women.

276 *Renew your character with nature and with art.* They say that one's condition changes every

seven years: let this change improve and heighten your taste. After the first seven years of life, we reach the age of reason; let a new perfection follow every seven years thereafter. Observe this natural variety and help it along, and expect others to improve also. This is why many changed their behavior or their estate, or their employment, and at times one does not notice until one sees how great the change has been. When you are twenty years old, you will be a peacock; at thirty, a lion; at forty, a camel; at fifty, a serpent; at sixty, a dog; at seventy, a monkey; and at eighty, nothing.

277 *Display your gifts*; show them off. There is a time for each one. Take advantage; no one can triumph every day. There are gallant people in whom what is little truly shines, and what is much shines bright enough to astonish. When you have both talent and a talent for displaying your gifts, the result is something prodigious. There are nations that know how to dazzle, and Spaniards do it better than anyone else. As soon as the world was created, there was light to show it off. Showing off satisfies, supplies what is missing, and gives everything a second being, even more so when it is grounded in reality. The heavens, which bestow perfection, encourage us to

display our gifts. You need skill to do so; even what is most excellent depends on circumstance and isn't always appropriate. Ostentation doesn't work when it is done out of season. Nor should we show off in an affected way, for ostentation borders on vanity, and vanity on scorn. It should be exercised with moderation, so as not to turn into vulgarity, and among wise men, an excessive display of one's gifts is not highly thought of. It often involves a certain silent eloquence, a bit of carelessness. Wise dissimulation is the best way to win praise, for privation awakens curiosity. It takes skill not to reveal all of your perfection at once, but to do so little by little, always adding a little more. Let one glorious occasion spur you on to another greater one, and the applause given to the first heighten expectation for the others.

278 *Don't call attention to yourself.* When others notice you doing so, your very gifts turn into defects and you will simply be left alone and criticized as an eccentric. Even beauty, if it is excessive, will harm your reputation. When it gives others pause, it is offensive, and disreputable eccentricities have the same effect, only greater. Some wish to be known for their vices, searching for new ways to discredit them-

selves. Even in matters of the understanding, excess produces pedantry.

279 *Don't answer those who contradict you.* Find out first whether they're being clever or simply vulgar. It isn't always stubbornness; sometimes it is a trick. So pay attention and don't get caught up in the former or cast down by the latter. No one demands more caution than a spy, and when someone has the skeleton key to minds, counter him by leaving the key of caution inside, on the other side of the keyhole.

280 *An honorable person.* Good conduct has departed, debts of gratitude now go unpaid, and few people give others the treatment they deserve. In all the world, the greatest services are now the least re-warded. There are entire nations inclined to treat others badly. From some, one fears treason; from others, inconstancy; from still others, deceit. Take notice of the bad behavior of others, not to imitate it but to defend yourself from it. Your own integrity can be ruined by the ruinous behavior of others. But the honorable man does not forget who he is because of what others are.

281 *Win favor from the intelligent.* The luke-warm "yes" of a truly singular person is worth more than the applause of the rabble. Why be pleased by the burps of bumpkins? The wise speak with under-standing, and their praise brings deathless satisfaction. Judicious Antigonus reduced the whole theater of his fame to Zeno alone,* and Plato took Aristotle for his entire school. Some want only to fill their bellies, even on vulgar fodder. Even sovereigns need people to write about them, and they fear their pens more than the ugly fear the brushes of the portrait painter.

282 *Use absence* to win respect or esteem. Presence diminishes fame, absence enlarges it. The absent person who was thought a lion turns into a mouse—ridiculous offspring of the mountain—when present. Gifts lose their sheen when they are handled: one sees the outer bark and not the spiritual pith. Imagination travels faster than sight. Deceit comes in through the ears, but usually leaves through the eyes. The person who retires into himself, into the

*Antigonus Gonatas, King of Macedonia, who greatly admired Zeno, founder of Stoic philosophy.

center of his reputation, preserves his good name. Even the Phoenix used absence to preserve its dignity and to turn desire into esteem.

283 *Be inventive, but sensibly.* Inventiveness reveals extreme intelligence, but who can be so without a touch of madness? Inventive people are ingenious; those who choose wisely, prudent. Inventiveness is also a grace, and very rare, for many are good at choosing, but few at wisely inventing, and these few went first, in excellence and in time. Novelty is flattering, and when successful, it makes what is good shine twice as much. In matters of judgment it is dangerous, for it involves paradox; in matters of intelligence, praiseworthy, and when both sorts are successful, they deserve applause.

284 *Mind your own business,* and you won't be slighted. Esteem yourself if you want esteem from others. Be stingy with yourself, not prodigal. Go where you're wanted, and you'll be well received. Never come unless you are called, never go unless you are sent. The person who commits himself on his own initiative brings hatred upon himself if he fails, and earns no gratitude when he succeeds. When you butt into things, you're the butt of scorn; if you meddle where you shouldn't, you'll be sent away in confusion.

285 *Don't perish on account of someone else's bad luck.* Know who is in trouble and expect him to call on you for help and mutual consolation. Misery loves company, and the miserable reach out their arms to those on whom they once turned their backs. Be careful when you try to save someone who is drowning. You can't help him without putting yourself in danger.

286 *Don't go completely into debt with anyone and everyone.* You will become a common slave. Some were born luckier than others; they can do good while others receive it. Freedom is more precious than the gift that makes us lose it. You should take greater pleasure in having many people depend on you than on depending on one person. The only advantage of having power is that you can do greater good. Above all, when you are given an obligation, don't take it as a favor. Most of the time it is the cleverness of others that has placed you in that position.

287 *Don't act when moved by passion*: you will get everything wrong. You cannot act for yourself if you are beside yourself, and passion always sends reason into exile. So find a prudent third party, one unmoved by passion. Onlookers always see more than those who are playing. When prudence feels emotion coming on, it is time to beat a hasty retreat. Otherwise, your blood will boil, you will do things bloodily, and a brief outburst will lead to many days of confusion and a loss of reputation.

288 *Adapt yourself to circumstance*. Governing, reasoning, and everything else must be done at the right moment. Want to do something when you can, for time and opportunity wait for no one. Don't live by generalities, unless it be to act virtuously, and don't ask desire to follow precise laws, for you will have to drink tomorrow from the water you scorn today. Some people are so paradoxically impertinent that they demand that circumstances adapt to their own whims, and help them succeed, rather than the other way around. But the wise know that the polestar of prudence lies in adapting themselves to the occasion.

289 *A man's worst disgrace: showing he is one*. Others stop seeing him as divine the day they see him very human. Levity is the greatest obstacle to reputation. The retiring person is held to be more than a person, and the light-headed are held to be less. No vice is more degrading, for levity is totally opposed to respectability. A light-headed man can have no substance, even less so when he is old, for age calls for prudence. And though this defect is common, it can lead to singular contempt.

290 *It is never a good idea to mix appreciation and affection*. To preserve respect, don't be loved too greatly. Love takes more liberties than hatred. Affection and veneration don't mix. Be neither very feared nor very loved. Love leads to familiarity, and casts out esteem. Be loved admiringly rather than affectionately.

291 *Know how to test others*. Let attentiveness and good judgment penetrate gravity and reserve. It takes great powers of judgment to measure someone

else's. It is more important to know the qualities and temperaments of people than those of stones and herbs. This is one of the subtlest things in life. Metals are identified by their sounds, and people by their speech. Words demonstrate integrity, and deeds even more so. Here is where one needs extraordinary care, profound observation, and critical power.

292 *Let your character be superior to the requirements of the job*, not vice versa. No matter how great the post, you must show you are greater. Deep talent grows even deeper, and more obvious, with each pursuit. The person with a narrow mind and heart will be easily caught, and eventually the weight of his duties will crush his reputation. The great Augustus was proud of being a better man than a prince. Here is where one needs a lofty spirit, and well-grounded confidence in oneself.

293 *Maturity*. It shines in the outer man, but even more in his customs. Material weight gives value to gold, and moral weight gives value to a person. It is the decorum that accompanies one's gifts, causing veneration. Composure is the façade of the

soul. It isn't the insensibility and stillness of fools, as silly people think, but a calm sense of authority. It speaks in wise sayings and deals in success. You are as much a true person as you are mature. When you stop behaving like a child and begin to be grave you acquire authority.

294 *Moderate your opinions*. Everyone forms his ideas according to his own interests, and offers abundant reasons to back them up. In most people, judgment yields to emotion. It often happens that two people meet head-on, and each presumes he is right. But reason is true, and never has two faces. In such encounters, proceed with wisdom and caution. Sometimes take the other side, and cautiously revise your own opinion. Examine your motives from the other's point of view. That way you will neither condemn him, nor justify yourself, so blindly.

295 *Not a braggart, but a doer*. They are proudest of their deeds who have least reason to be so. They turn everything into mystery, and do it without grace: chameleons of applause, providing bellyfuls of laughter. Vanity was always annoying, but

this sort is laughed at. Some people are like beggars of deeds, little ants piling up honor. You should show the least vanity about your greatest gifts. Content yourself with doing: leave saying to others. Give deeds away, don't sell them. And don't rent golden quills so that others can write mud, offending common sense. Try to be heroic rather than merely seem so.

296 *A man of majestic gifts.* The greatest gifts make the greatest man. One great gift surpasses a mediocre multitude. A certain person wanted all his things to be large, even his ordinary utensils. Great people should strive for great spiritual gifts. In God all is infinite, all immense; and thus in a hero all must be grand and majestic, so that all his actions and even his words can be dressed in transcendent majesty.

297 *Always behave as though others were watching.* A man who looks after his actions sees that others see him, or will. He knows that walls have ears, and that what is badly done is bursting to become known. Even when he is alone he behaves as though all the world were watching, and knows that all will be revealed. He behaves as though he already had

witnesses: those who, when they hear something, will be so later. The person who wanted everyone to see him didn't care when people searched his house while sitting in their own.

298 *Three things make a marvel*, and are at the acme of true nobility: fertile intelligence, deep powers of judgment, and a pleasant, relevant taste. Imagination is a great gift, but it is greater still to reason well and understand the good. The intelligence should be sharp, not laborious. It should reside in the head, not the backbone. When one is twenty, the will reigns; at thirty, the intelligence; at forty, judgment. There are understandings that throw off light, like the eyes of the lynx, and they reason best in the greatest darkness. There are others who always hit upon what is most relevant. Things occur to them often and well. O happy fertile wit! As for good taste, it seasons one's entire life.

299 *Leave people hungry*. Leave nectar on their lips. Esteem is measured in desire. As with thirst, it is good to allay it but not to quench it. The good, if little, is twice good. Things fall off sharply the second time around. Bellyfuls of pleasure are dangerous: they cause even the most eternal eminence to be scorned. The one rule for pleasing: whet the appetite, keep people hungry. The impatience of desire will do more than the ennui of enjoyment, and waiting deepens our pleasure.

300 *In a word, be a saint; that says everything.* Virtue is a chain of all perfections, the center of all happiness. She makes you prudent, discreet, shrewd, sensible, wise, brave, cautious, honest, happy, praiseworthy, true . . . a universal hero. Three things make one blessed: saintliness, wisdom, and prudence. Virtue is the sun of the lesser world, and its hemisphere is a good conscience. It is so lovely that it wins God's grace and that of others. There is nothing as lovable as virtue, nor as hateful as vice. Virtue alone is for real; all else is sham. Talent and greatness depend on virtue, not on fortune. Only virtue is sufficient unto herself. She makes us love the living and remember the dead.

1. All has reached perfection, and becoming a true person is the greatest perfection of all.
2. Character and intelligence.
3. Keep matters in suspense.
4. Knowledge and courage take turns at greatness.
5. Make people depend on you.
6. Reach perfection.
7. Don't outshine your boss.
8. Not to be swayed by passions: the highest spiritual quality of all.
9. Avoid the defects of your country.
10. Fame and fortune.
11. Associate with those you can learn from.
12. Nature and art, material and labor.
13. Act on the intentions of others: their ulterior and superior motives.
14. Both reality and manner.
15. Surround yourself with auxiliary wits.
16. Knowledge and honorable intentions.
17. Keep changing your style of doing things.
18. Application and capacity.
19. When you start something, don't raise other people's expectations.
20. A person born in the right age.
21. The art of success.

22. Be well informed.
23. Don't have a single imperfection.
24. Temper your imagination.
25. Know how to take a hint.
26. Find each person's "handle," his weak point.
27. Better to be intensive than extensive.
28. Be vulgar in nothing.
29. Be righteous and firm.
30. Don't occupy yourself with disreputable things.
31. Know the fortunate in order to choose them, and the unfortunate in order to flee from them.
32. Be known for pleasing others.
33. Know when to put something aside.
34. Know your best quality.
35. Weigh matters carefully.
36. Take the measure of your luck.
37. Know what insinuation is, and how to use it.
38. Quit while you're ahead.
39. Know when things are at their acme, when they are ripe, and know how to take advantage of them.
40. Grace in dealing with others.
41. Never exaggerate.
42. Born to rule.
43. Feel with the few, speak with the many.
44. Sympathy with the great.

45. Use, but don't abuse, hidden intentions.
46. Temper your antipathy.
47. Avoid committing yourself to risky enterprises.
48. You are as much a real person as you are deep.
49. A person of sharp observation and sound judgment.
50. Never lose your self-respect.
51. Know how to choose.
52. Never lose your composure.
53. Be diligent and intelligent.
54. Act boldly but prudently.
55. Know how to wait.
56. Think on your feet.
57. Thoughtful people are safer.
58. Adapt to those around you.
59. End well.
60. Good judgment.
61. Eminence in what is best.
62. Use the best instruments.
63. The excellence of being first.
64. Avoid grief.
65. Elevated taste.
66. Take care to make things turn out well.
67. Choose an occupation in which you can win praise.
68. Make others understand.

69. Don't give in to every common impulse.
70. Know how to say "no."
71. Don't be inconsistent, either because of temperament or out of affectation.
72. Be resolute.
73. Know when to be evasive.
74. Don't be unfriendly.
75. Choose a heroic model.
76. Don't always be joking.
77. Adapt yourself to everyone else.
78. Skill at trying things out.
79. A jovial character.
80. Be careful when you inform yourself about things.
81. Renew your brilliance.
82. Neither all bad nor all good.
83. Allow yourself some venial fault.
84. Know how to use your enemies.
85. Don't be the wild card.
86. Head off rumor.
87. Culture and refinement.
88. Deal with others in a grand way.
89. Know yourself.
90. The art of living long: live well.
91. Never act unless you think it prudent to do so.
92. Transcendent wisdom.
93. A universal man.

94. Unfathomable gifts.
95. Keep expectations alive.
96. Good common sense.
97. Make your reputation and keep it.
98. Write your intentions in cipher.
99. Reality and appearance.
100. A man free of deceit and illusion.
101. Half the world is laughing at the other half, and folly rules over all.
102. A stomach for big helpings of fortune.
103. To each, the dignity that befits him.
104. Have a good sense of what each job requires.
105. Don't be tiresome.
106. Don't flaunt your good fortune.
107. Don't look self-satisfied.
108. A shortcut to becoming a true person.
109. Don't berate others.
110. Don't wait to be a setting sun.
111. Have friends.
112. Win the goodwill of others.
113. Plan for bad fortune while your fortune is good.
114. Never compete.
115. Get used to the failings of your friends, family, and acquaintances.
116. Always deal with people of priciple.
117. Don't talk about yourself.
118. Be known for your courtesy.

119. Don't make yourself disliked.
120. Live practically.
121. Don't make much ado about nothing.
122. Mastery in words and deeds.
123. A person without affectation.
124. Make yourself wanted.
125. Don't be a blacklist of others' faults.
126. The fool isn't someone who does something foolish, but the one who doesn't know how to conceal it.
127. Ease and grace in everything.
128. Highmindedness.
129. Never complain.
130. Do, but also seem.
131. A gallant spirit.
132. Reconsider.
133. Better to be mad with everyone than sane all alone.
134. Double your store of life's necessities.
135. Don't have the spirit of contradiction.
136. Size up the matter.
137. The wise are sufficient unto themselves.
138. Leave things alone.
139. Know your unlucky days.
140. Go straight to the good in everything.
141. Don't listen to yourself.
142. Don't defend the wrong side out of stubbornness.

143. Don't be paradoxical to avoid being vulgar.
144. Enter conceding and come out winning.
145. Hide your wounded finger.
146. Look deep inside.
147. Don't be inaccessible.
148. Be skilled in conversation.
149. Let someone else take the hit.
150. Know how to sell your wares.
151. Think ahead.
152. Don't keep company with those who will make you seem less gifted.
153. Don't step into the huge gap left by someone else.
154. Neither quick to believe, nor quick to love.
155. Skill at mastering your passions.
156. Select your friends.
157. Don't be mistaken about people.
158. Know how to use your friends.
159. Know how to suffer fools.
160. Speak prudently.
161. Know your own sweet faults.
162. Conquer envy and malevolence.
163. Don't let your sympathy for the unfortunate make you one of them.
164. Float a trial balloon.
165. Wage a clean war.
166. Distinguish the man of words from the man of deeds.

167. Be self-reliant.
168. Don't become a monster of foolishness.
169. Better to avoid missing once than to hit the mark a hundred times.
170. In all matters, keep something in reserve.
171. Don't waste the favors people owe you.
172. Never compete with someone who has nothing to lose.
173. Don't be made of glass in your dealings with others.
174. Don't live in a hurry.
175. A person of substance.
176. Either know, or listen to someone who does.
177. Don't grow too familiar with others.
178. Trust your heart.
179. Reserve is the seal of talent.
180. Never govern yourself by what your enemy ought to do.
181. Don't lie, but don't tell the whole truth.
182. Show everyone a bit of daring: an important sort of prudence.
183. Don't hold on to anything too firmly.
184. Don't stand on ceremony.
185. Don't risk your reputation on one roll of the dice.
186. Know when something is a defect.
187. When something pleases others, do it yourself. When it is odious, have someone else do it.

188. Find something to praise.
189. Utilize other people's privations.
190. Find consolation in everything.
191. Don't take payment in politeness.
192. A peaceable person is a long-lived one.
193. Beware of someone who pretends to put your interest before his own.
194. Be realistic about yourself and your own affairs.
195. Know how to appreciate.
196. Know your lucky star.
197. Never stumble over fools.
198. Know how to transplant yourself.
199. Be prudent when you try to win esteem.
200. Have something to hope for.
201. Fools are all those who look like fools, and half of those who do not.
202. Words and deeds make a perfect man.
203. Know the great men of your age.
204. Undertake the easy as though it were difficult, and the difficult as though it were easy.
205. Learn to use scorn.
206. Know that there are vulgar people everywhere.
207. Use self-control.
208. Don't die from an attack of foolishness.
209. Free yourself from common foolishness.
210. Know how to handle truth.

211. In heaven all is contentment, in hell all is sorrow, and on earth, which is in between, we find both.
212. Never reveal the final stratagems of your art.
213. Know how to contradict.
214. Don't turn one act of foolishness into two.
215. Pay attention to the person with hidden intentions.
216. Express yourself clearly.
217. Neither love nor hate forever.
218. Never do something out of stubbornness, only out of attentive reflection.
219. Don't be known for your artifice.
220. If you can't wear the skin of a lion, wear the skin of a fox.
221. Don't be hotheaded.
222. Cautious hesitation is a sign of prudence.
223. Don't be eccentric.
224. Know how to take things.
225. Know your major defect.
226. Be sure to win people's favor.
227. Don't surrender to first impressions.
228. Don't be a scandal sheet.
229. Parcel out your life wisely.
230. Open your eyes before it is too late.
231. Never show half-finished things to others.
232. Have a touch of the practical.
233. Don't mistake other people's tastes.

234. If you trust your honor to someone else, keep his in pledge.
235. Know how to ask.
236. Turn someone's reward into a favor.
237. Never share your secrets with those greater than you.
238. Know what piece you are missing.
239. Don't be overly clever.
240. Make use of folly.
241. Allow yourself to be joked about, but don't joke about others.
242. Follow through on your victories.
243. Don't be all dove.
244. Place others in your debt.
245. Sometimes you should reason with uncommon sense.
246. Don't give explanations to those who haven't asked for them.
247. Know a little more, live a little less.
248. Don't be obsessed with the latest.
249. Don't start living when you should be ending.
250. When should we reason backward?
251. Use human means as though divine ones didn't exist, and divine means as though there were no human ones.
252. Live neither entirely for yourself nor entirely for others.

253. Don't express your ideas too clearly.
254. Don't scorn an evil because it is a small one.
255. Know how to do good.
256. Be prepared.
257. Stop short of breaking off.
258. Look for someone to help bear your misfortunes.
259. Foresee affronts and turn them into favors.
260. You can't belong entirely to others, and no one can be entirely yours.
261. Don't persist in folly.
262. Know how to forget.
263. Many pleasant things are better when they belong to someone else.
264. Don't have days when you are careless.
265. Get those who depend on you into tough situations.
266. Don't be bad by being too good.
267. Silken words, delivered gently.
268. The wise do sooner what fools do later.
269. Take advantage of your novelty.
270. Don't be the only one to condemn what is popular.
271. If you know little, stick to what is surest in each profession.
272. Add courtesy to the price of what you're selling.
273. Understand the characters of the people you are dealing with.

274. Be charming.
275. Row with the current, but preserve your dignity.
276. Renew your character with nature and with art.
277. Display your gifts.
278. Don't call attention to yourself.
279. Don't answer those who contradict you.
280. An honorable person.
281. Win favor from the intelligent.
282. Use absence.
283. Be inventive, but sensibly.
284. Mind your own business.
285. Don't perish on account of someone else's bad luck.
286. Don't go completely into debt with anyone and everyone.
287. Don't act when moved by passion.
288. Adapt yourself to circumstance.
289. A man's worst disgrace: showing he *is* one.
290. It is never a good idea to mix appreciation and affection.
291. Know how to test others.
292. Let your character be superior to the requirements of the job.
293. Maturity.
294. Moderate your opinions.
295. Not a braggart, but a doer.
296. A man of majestic gifts.

297. Always behave as though others were watching.
298. Three things make a marvel . . .
299. Leave people hungry.
300. In a word, be a saint; that says everything.